POETRY AGAINST ALL

a diary

JOHANNES GÖRANSSON

Tarpaulin Sky Press
Chicago, IL
Saxtons River, VT
2020

Poetry Against All: A Diary
© 2020 Johannes Göransson
ISBN-13: 978-1-939460-23-3
Printed and bound in the USA

Tarpaulin Sky Press
P.O. Box 189
Grafton, Vermont 05146
TarpaulinSky.com

For more information on Tarpaulin Sky Press trade paperback and hand-
bound editions, as well as information regarding distribution, personal
orders, and catalogue requests, please visit our website at tarpaulinsky.com.

POETRY AGAINST ALL

OPENING

Why do I always cry when I hear this Adele song on airplanes? Such an absurd song: the speaker returns to the lover of her youth and pleads with him to go with her. Go where? Back to "summer" of course, when they were young. Only now the it's covered with ants. Why go back to summer? There's only one thing to do in summer when it's no longer summer: kill yourself.

Flowers: I'm going home to write a book about corpses and children. I'm writing in the ruins of summer. I'm writing a rotten poem. A rotten summer is the proper place for melancholics and emigrants. An expired summer looks like a crime scene: the ants are crawling in the folds of a dead swan's plumage.

"An airplane is a paranoid symbol." These words pop into my head as I watch the rabble around me. They're all watching war movies. I'm watching a war movie. It looks like it's about conquest but I can't understand the words. Speak louder, I'm looking for the secret of this violent thing. I'm writing a poem in its language, but it takes place in a rotten summer, a toxic zone where all desires are materialized.

I'm going back home to write a book about sugar. I'm writing it with sugar on my fingers. The ants love this kind of poetry. "Summer poetry." Dead swan poetry. Ruin poetry. Sugar poetry. I was named after this song: Baby Blue. This is a cover. You must leave now. The New Economy always tells us to leave the dead summer, the ruins, but I can't. This is a cover. I was named after the original. It was not the original. There is no original baby. There is no original blue.

Dear Adele, I'm going home to write a book about summer even though it's September and no longer summer and I'm married and I have kids. But I love the haze of summer. I've been poisoned by it. I have a summer disease. Outside of summer rages the New Economy, which is starting to sound old in the era of the New End. I'm writing a book about corpses and summer. I'm opening up my body with the spear of a gladiolus.

DAY 1

I've spent hours just wandering around Copenhagen. This city is like a copy of Sweden but the language is slightly off. I can barely understand it anymore. I've heard a home is always a fantasy. I'm writing a pervert's book.

When Martin left to give his lecture at the university, I sat down on this futon and looked around. Saw a book with a striking cover: a black-and-white photograph of three young women naked, one of them wearing Mary Janes, each of them holding a photograph of a face in front of their faces. The photographs are sexual but not pornographic. They don't allow the pornographic gaze to settle. The figures are masked, opaque at the same time as they are private. Foreign and familiar. Perhaps it brings me into a zone where such binaries break down. The book is photographs by Francesca Woodman.

Felt like my face had a kind luster today as I walked around. I wanted to own Copenhagen. But I also felt like someone was following me. Perhaps a kind of angel who mistook me for someone dead. It's an easy mistake, I've made it several times since coming here. I want to own Copenhagen, but I promised the angel I would never return. You and whose army was its reply. I thought about Francesca Woodman disappearing into the wallpaper. A feminine army was what I told myself.

What would be the first thing I would do if I owned Copenhagen? Change its name. Burn down the tower which I so long to inhabit. I think it's part of a hospital. The Hospital of Innocence: We go there to cure us of our virginities. Inside, the past comes back. Refuses to stay dead. I would never leave. That's why I have to burn it down. I will never leave. I'm always the one in the tower. It's why I'm such a virgin.

I'm sitting in a café in Copenhagen reading Saul Friedlander's *Reflections of Nazism: An Essay on Kitsch and Death*. Friedlander writes so beautifully about the doomed atmosphere of the Nazi and Nazi-evocative artworks that it feels like he's taken in by this aesthetic of "debased romanticism." He writes about an "overload of symbols" and a "baroque setting" and "mysterious atmosphere." He seems to be describing Francesca Woodman.

When Romanticism is "debased," it is corrupted, made kitsch. It's "atmosphere" instead of meaning, mood over substance. It's "overloaded": there's too much of it. But isn't Romanticism always kitsch: with its bird songs, its shepherds, its idiot boys. I'm not interested in any poetry that isn't Romantic. I'm not interested in any Romanticism that isn't debased.

The only way Friedlander feels he can write about these "ravishing images" is to make himself vulnerable to their power. To let the images "ravish" him. The book as an experiment in masochistic erotics. I think of John Donne: Holy Sonnet 14 is not addressed to God, it's addressed to Art. I'm following the same masochistic logic with this going-home BS. With this prancing around in the Zone.

4

I've made myself vulnerable to Woodman. I'm carrying her around with me.

The opposite of making oneself vulnerable to the ravishing images of art is to reject "retinal" art in favor of a concept, a thesis. Conceptual poetry makes the poet into such a clean figure of strength: art becomes a "corpse," something abject, grotesque. This is why they are constantly repeating the claim that they've killed poetry. Taking its cue from a Christian division between spirit and body, Conceptual poetry posits a binary model: concept and retinal, gold standard and inflation. This is why Kenny Goldsmith, Vanessa Place so often justify their work by saying that there's too much kitschy poetry. They are the gold standard, the rest of poetry is mass produced, indistinct, excessive, tasteless. In this way they strangely recuperate the very traditional model of authorship they have made their reputation from criticizing: the Great Original who stands out from the imitative masses.

In this rejection of "ravishing" art, the Conceptualists are strangely compatible with the Quietist poetics they so despise. The fundamental rule of Quietist aesthetics is to reject all things "ravishing" as immoral, as too much. Quietism is an aesthetic or—perhaps more so—a pedagogy based on moderation. As with the Conceptualists, the idealization of moderation is a matter of economics: the fear inflation will corrupt their interiorities. Turn authenticity into kitsch.

There's a tautology at the heart of Friedlander's argument: art is that which makes you susceptible to art. That which generates more art. Art makes copies of itself. In the reader. These "ravishing images" continually proliferate, calling for more. Kitsch is in the excess of art. It urges us to mimic, to make more. Another word for this possession is Beauty.

In Francesca Woodman's photographs I am wounded. The photograph as wound and wounding. Is this Catholic art? Am I a saint?

If I had to make a self-portrait in Copenhagen, what kind of portrait would it be? It couldn't be a Woodman photograph because I'm always outside. Perhaps something more like Wojnarowicz's hustlers with Rimbaud masks: photographs that should be revealing if it weren't for the mask. Photographs of injecting a drug or receiving a blowjob in some ruins. Selfies of the outside becoming inside, the inside pouring out. Selfies of the self becoming strange. Becoming Art. That way I wouldn't be such a stranger here. But I wouldn't belong either.

The Sugar Book is a work of debased romanticism. I'm here with my camera eyes and catastrophes. It's fall. We are the aftermath. The road of excess is lined with road kill. I'm wearing my Orpheus mask and I'm not even home yet. But I can see it from across the sound, across the water. I will walk to you on my knees.

DAY 2

Couldn't sleep. Watched that scene in Tarkovsky's *The Mirror* when the boy wakes up and sees his father washing his mother's hair and then the sound of an ocean liner and then the water begins to pour out of the ceiling and walls and then mother sways like some horror movie and then the whole thing collapses. Thought about my own children. Thought about the way things collapse: first you hear it.

nice TRANSITION

Listened to Geechie Wiley's "Last Kind Words Blues": The lover is a ghost coming back from a foreign war. She sees him coming across the fields like a ghost, across the river. Her brings her flowers, broken nails. She lets the buzzards eat his corpse. His body is now foreign. This is how you treat a foreign body.

Wrote a "kill text for underage fans" like a violation of the insipid innocence that permeates America's myths about itself. Thought about Michael Savitz's poem about wearing a "swimsuit" as he crawls back to his grandparents. Must be the most perverse quotation marks I've ever read. Thought about the rubber gloves of Abu Ghraib and the rubber gloves of Cocteau's Orpheus movie. Thought about those rubber gloves as being in quotation marks in my sugar book. Remembered that right wing radio guy saying that Abu Ghraib was no worse than NEA winners. As if people objected to the aesthetics of the torture, not the murder. Thought about the word torso. Thought of how Basquiat uses the torso. Torso: the word feel inherently violent. I want to take a photograph of it. The camera makes quotations. The source text is disgusting.

Martin asked me if I thought Olga Ravn was gurlesque. I opened her book *I Eat Myself Like Heather. Girl Mind* to a random page and read: "The gold hearts, purple party shrouds all through life, the boundary has been crossed, now we will have to learn to take pleasure in that too, an easy-to-read book with the title sex sucks cement in hell. // The gold hearts, the girl room, solved the mystery by saying hey we DIDN'T solve it." I told him yes. When he asked me to define the gurlesque, I told him it has to do with kitsch, violence, girlhood—poisoning oneself with poetry. Subjecting one's deer heart to Art.

Martin is working on an essay connecting contemporary US conceptual writing to Reznikoff and the Holocaust. For the conceptualists, all images must be eliminated. All "retinal" poetry is "dead." So many extravagant corpses everywhere. The poem is the most extravagant waste, as Bataille wrote. Poetry and mourning cults, as Bataille wrote. Poems are so many corpses. I want to write *The Sugar Book* about them.

DAY 3

Is Woodman kitsch? Romanticism? Is she gurlesque? What does she have to do with Hans Bellmer's crime-scenes-as-erotic-art? Hans Bellmer's doll wears those same Mary Janes. Is it knowledge of her suicide that brings that doomed sheen to Woodman's photography, or is it true what they say about photography, that it is always about death?

Or is it the case that photography makes kitsch out of everything, makes us into foreigners, spectators, voyeurs, as we gaze at these lovely private vignettes? Or is it simply that art is the poison. And we are the ribcage.

The photographs of Woodman and Bellmer both take place in the aftermath. In a private space, the photograph both registers the crime and somehow is the crime, the poison. It taints the space by turning it into Art, images, corpses. Art as murder mysteries that are never solved. The corpse makes the setting baroque. The atmosphere is always overwhelming.

What I love about murder mysteries are the crime scenes. All those disparate objects brought together in one scene is like a surrealist assemblage. They have a mysterious atmosphere, in which the killer lurks. To solve the crime means to create a narrative that makes sense of the assemblage, removes its mystery. The narrative clears the atmosphere, turns the killer into a person who can be prosecuted, establishes the guilt (in the interiority of the killer or in wider political conflict) through causality. I'm not interested in guilt. That's about balancing the accounts. Balancing the account is the opposite of art. Art should be ravishing images.

Henning Mankell's Wallander mysteries have the most evocative crime scenes: swans are set on fire, a young woman sets herself on fire in a rape field, a group of young people are dressed in 17th-century garb. Wallander is capable of finding the killers because he loves opera. Because he's an alcoholic, a diabetic, coming apart. His body is vulnerable to art and intoxication, it is breaking down. He has the sugar sickness.

Wallander's father is similar to Wallander: he's tainted by art. He's an artist who keeps repeating the same painting— an idiot Warhol (or the idiot Warhol always liked to pretend he was)—as if he had no memory. By the end of the series the father is dead, the daughter has taken Wallander's place as detective and Wallander has Alzheimer's, the narrative disappearing again. The parasite of art has used up Wallander—the man and the series.

It's like the protagonist in *Stalker*: Art's forbidden zone has turned his hair gray in patches and has contaminated his sperms, causing his only child to be born deformed but magical. The relationship between guide, detective and poet evokes for me someone who works with atmospheres and mysteries. It's why the main character in *The Sugar Book* is all of these.

The atmosphere is the killer. That's why the detective only catches glimpses of the killer at first. The killer is not yet a person. The detective has to use narrative make a whole person out of the glimpses, the atmosphere, so that he can turn art into a crime that can be tried in court.

Never balance the accounts.

DAY 4

I'm writing about an aftermath. All poetry takes place in the aftermath, where everyone belongs but are also out of place. I want my book to be torn into pieces. It's why I'm rewriting this book with my shitty Orpheus mask on. My rubber mask and my rubber gloves. My book is about fashion. For example plague masks.

> The cadaver is its own image. It no longer entertains any relation with this world where it still appears except that of an image, an obscure possibility, a shadow ever present behind the living form, which now far from separating itself from this form transforms it entirely into shadow the corpse is a reflection becoming master of the life it reflects—absorbing it identifying substantively with it by moving it from its use value and from its truth value to something incredible—something neutral which there is no getting used to and if the cadaver is so similar it is because it is at a certain moment similarity par excellence altogether similarity and also nothing more it is the likeness like to an absolute degree overwhelming and marvelous but what is it like nothing.
>
> —Maurice Blanchot[1]

I'm thinking about JG Ballard's *Crash*: The scene where the narrator has been in a crash and he sits buckled up in his car, looking at the corpse on his hood, and on the other side of

---
[1] Translated by Lydia Davis.

12

the corpse is the corpse's wife, also buckled in, also looking at the corpse. It's almost a parody of Blanchot (it's literally a corpse). Almost a parody of all that talk condemning the "spectator" as "passive" (and therefore immoral, therefore like Plato's cave dwellers). Almost a parody of the movies (the ultimate cave for fantasies). As in the movies, the two spectators seem to catch something with their eyes, the car-death-sexuality obsessions enters through their eyes. This is how art works: through infection, contamination. I catch Art.

The logic of *The Sugar Book* has to be contaminatory because the foreigner has no interiority and in the Los Angeles of *The Sugar Book* we are all foreigners. We go to the movies to find a home but it's not there anymore. That's what the movies tell us. They lie. It was never there. *Solaris*.

Foreigners make the best detectives, but they also make the best killers. They have no souls, portrayed as flat. This allows them to move in the volatility of atmosphere. This is also why the foreigner is kitsch. I take a selfie. Insects and electricity.

DAY 5

It seems for Friedlander, rather than a political movement, Nazism becomes an idea of art: excess, intoxication, proliferation, inflation. It's the sublime but in bad taste. The shitty sublime. Why is it shitty? Because it's about history but it's also beautiful. Because we keep looking, instead of "living."

There is no cure for looking at images. At least that's what they would have us believe. The degenerate porn addicts keep looking at pictures of naked bodies. An underworld of bodies and flowers: The poet must be a pornographer. No the poet must make pornography against porn.

In *Distant Star* by Roberto Bolaño: The climax is when all the fascists go into the photography show and come out puking. But we don't see the photographs. We just see the effect, the vomiting. The exhibit is like a black hole in the middle of the book: it both explains everything that happens and refused to actually show anything. Of course the photographer is a poet. The character is a poet-as-pornographer. But Bolaño's book—with its black room at the center of the book, a center that cannot be seen but whose effects is vomiting—is a work of parapornography: the pornography vomits itself.

H.M. asked me: Why do you always have to ruin your poems?

My poems are always ruined by the sex.

And by my pathological homesickness.

I can't be saved from all these fantasies.

I'm always away.

Always writing on this poem about foxgloves, hemlock, *thousandbeauties*.

DAY 6

The word "tusensköner": The correct translation is "daisies." Daisies. Ann Jäderlund would never write a poem with "daisies" in it. Her poems are teeming with thousandbeauties.

The words "baroque" and "ruins," which play such a central role to Friedlander's notion of Nazi kitsch, are replayed in all the discussions in the US right now about "ruin porn." Ravishing pictures of luxurious ruins: Is it the fact that the ruins are mostly formerly wealthy buildings that makes the ruin porn luxurious, or is it the ruination process, the debasing process that is the ultimate luxury?

These ruin-porn buildings always strike me as toxic spaces. The toxicity of art.

With a stunning frequency, ruin porn is condemned in xenophobic terms. The photographers are accused of being foreigners, or worse, foreign tourists. I'm reading a discussion right now, where one accused photographer points out that he's actually from Detroit. A critic immediately replies: "No, if you were really from Detroit you wouldn't aestheticize our economic collapse."

Not only is it only foreigners who make "porn," making porn seems to make you into a foreigner.

What is lost in the foreign? The currency of interiority. The communication of interiority. Without communication, language and bodies proliferate, become noisy. Foreigners lead to inflation: too many people, too many versions, not enough soul. Or: Too many images, too many ghosts, pornography. The foreigner traffics in pornography. The foreigner is always looking at life from a distance, but it's not a safe distance. The foreigner's distance is perverse. The foreigner is turned on. The foreigner makes the natural strange. The foreigner has secrets, but no humanity. The foreigner takes your photo, makes an image out of you.

Francesca Woodman makes a mask of me.

Francesca Woodman makes my body feel foreign to me.

That time D. [an "experimental writer" from the Bay Area] attacked me for turning her book into pornography by reading it retinally and failing to see it as an ethical "critique" of pornography.

Later she forbade me from writing about her writing because I come from "some place different." I'm not from the Bay Area. I'm from some place else. A foreigner, I made pornography out of even her moral critique. I ruined her sense of agency. I made kitsch out of her experimental art. As Haryette Mullen might have put it, I was an "unimagined reader." I perverted her book. She had to throw me out of her Republic (because I was not a member already). She wanted to denaturalize me.

Tarkovsky's *Stalker* must be one of the origins of "ruin porn." The images are so beautiful—so "ravishing"—they verge on kitsch. The snow falling indoors, the reliquary of discarded objects under water. The imagery is so gorgeous, iconophilic. I just want to look and look.

When I went to Detroit I slept in motel with blood on the pillow. Outside my window: a crumbling facade. I read poetry for the ruins because they reminded me of *Stalker*, where the guide brings customers into the Zone, which may be the area infected by a toxic disaster or may be the Zone of Art, where every desire can come true. The guide's hair is gray in tufts and his child was born misshapen because he has spent too much time in Art's evil zone; it has made him an outsider in his town, a foreigner in his own family. Art affects the body like cancer. Home is where your heart is, homesick is what your heart is. What evil it is to be so saturated by art's strangeness.

Everything needs to break. It's hard to think about writing and not think about skin.

DAY 7

The word 'nostalgia' comes from two Greek roots: νόστος, nós-tos ('return home') and ἄλγος, álgos ('longing'). I would define it as a longing for a home that no longer exists or has never existed. Nostalgia is a sentiment of loss and displacement, but it is also a romance with one's own phantasy. Nostalgic love can only survive in a long-distance relationship. A cinematic image of nostalgia is a double exposure, or a superimposition of two images—of home and abroad, of past and present, of dream and everyday life. The moment we try to force it into a single image, it breaks the frame or burns the surface.

—Svetlana Boym

You can't long for a place that still exists. The worst is to be in the place and yet to long for it. This paradox transforms me into a ghost. No, I was already a ghost. Since I was 13 years old I've been a ghost. And America has tried to exorcise me. But not as hard as I've tried. I'm trying right now. It's finally working.

How strange it is to be home. Seeing this place where I grew up is oddly similar to the sensation of going to Korea. The feeling of returning home and the feeling of being some place utterly foreign, belonging and strangeness: How can these feelings be so similar? Something between joy and melancholia. A head-on crash with fantasies.

I think about the day in Seoul when I almost lost it. All the food was too flavorful, there were photographs of meat on all the walls, the air was full of food odors, an octopus struggled to get out of an aquarium, I ran into the museum of contemporary art as if this would provide the foreigner with a neutral space, but when I put the headphones on in the exhibit of multimedia art I heard "contamination" and "virginity" over and over. Back at the hotel Yideum bought me bottle of makli, which we drank with abandon.

What did I do with all those diaristic entries I wrote in Seoul, all night when I couldn't sleep, when I was going insane, when I kept thinking about the octopus in the aquarium, when I transcribed the voices from that exhibition. I wish I had it. Wish I could insert it into *The Sugar Book*. This was where I began to write *The Sugar Book*. In that museum, where voices told me about bodies, mediumicity, aftermath.

I'm staying with Thomas for a few days before I move in to the apartment I've rented in Malmö. Thomas has bought the house his parents lived in when we were kids, but he's totally remodeled it. Very stylish. He certainly has good taste, but then teaching good (modern) taste to the working class was a key component of the Social Democrats' "non-bloody revolution" in the middle of the century.

How does Tarkovsky's *Solaris* end? Isn't it with the illusion that his home has somehow fantastically been maintained. Never ruined. Is this why I've always thought the ending is so sad? There is something choking about a past that remains in tact, a fantasy that is physicalized.

I think about Paul Celan's poem about remembering Paris. It's only after they gamble away their eyes and hair, after it rains inside their ruined hotel room (the way it snows inside buildings in *Stalker*), that they are finally dead and can breathe. "We were finally dead and could breathe." It's the most beautiful poem I know, a ghostly poem, a melancholic poem about tourism, ruins.

DAY 8

It's difficult to think about Thomas having a whole life after I left Sweden. It feels like an affront. Some of these other people from my childhood: For them, I'm probably just a shadowy person who disappeared in 7th grade never to return. Most of them won't even remember that I existed. I'm also humiliated knowing that they've forgotten me, because I haven't forgotten them. I remember every single one of them. The one exception is the girl with the short haircut, Maria Nilsson. When I think of her I just see Joyelle's face.

If art is a house, it has many mansions, fallen down mansions. Francesca Woodman is almost naked, the snake is almost real. I'm in there with her, shooting an ad for a brilliant kind of perfume. It's a hyacinth perfume. They call me the hyacinth girl because of my delicate hands, they make a mess with the flowers.

I'm sleeping in the bedroom that used to be Thomas's bedroom, but now Linea—his oldest daughter, a track-and-field athlete—sleeps in here. It's weird to sleep in these teenage sheets and know that this is where I watched one of the only pornos I've ever watched, *American Taboo 3* (mainly I remember the bathtub scene).

On her nightstand Linnea has a fashion magazine with a brilliant green-painted face on the cover. Fashion can be fantastic—everything could be made of mother-of-pearl—but poetry has to be restrained because any kind of excess is a threat to our model of interiority, the gold standard of meaningfulness. In this way we can dismiss the sensational as frivolous, belonging to the debased and utterly retinal domain of fashion. I write for the senses. In US poetry the senses are always at risk of becoming pornographic. *Sensationalistic.*

Like when S. [critic and professor] said I was "tossing bombs" into US poetry. Being sensationalistic. Being a flat foreigner. Being violence.

What is Francesca Woodman's relationship to fashion photography? I keep thinking about Woodman, pulling up her photographs on the Internet. I love the blurring of the body, how it moves through the abandoned mansion. She seems both utterly passive and incredibly energetic, driven by a calm but intensive force. Not interiority but saturation. Not privacy but atmosphere. She has a gothic allure. The atmosphere is ravishing.

I think about Wojnarowicz's photos of Rimbaud in NYC. The distinction between private and public, interior and exterior are volatilized. This is why I wear masks when I write about the family in *The Sugar Book*. My mask is made of crinoline.

DAY 9

Instead of interiority, Woodman has secrets. She is overloaded with secrets.

In David Lynch's *Twin Peaks*, Laura Palmer is "full of secrets." The more the detectives look into her past, the more things they find out. Her secrets are excessive, they cannot possibly be contained in a person's life, in a person's interiority. She becomes a double. Something foreign. An image. And ends up screaming in the underworld. She is a force of excess: both as riddle and scream. She's either inaudibly whispering or too loud in the red room. The only way to understand her is by going into the cinematic underworld. To be locked up there for 20 years. In the baroque room with the red velvet curtains, the zigzag floor pattern. The overloaded atmosphere.

There's something decadent about riddles. They always threaten to generate excess, to fail to anchor the imagery, become unredeemed imagery, become kitsch. How many times have I heard poets pointificate: Poems should not be riddles because they should be "accessible." Riddles are not poems because they contain secrets. But it's exactly the sense of a secret that makes them poetic, fascinating. I'm intrigued by Laura Palmer, by Francesca Woodman. The riddle that cannot be solved: it leads me into the red room movie theater.

I want to watch Tarkovsky's movies as if they were made by Woodman. I want to dream about her mansion when I write my sugar book. The poems will take place in mansions, in red rooms, in afterlives, in movie theaters. Prom queens surrounded by snakes will whisper their pornography. I will scream and scream. I already have a secret object. I keep it close at all times. My passport, dummy.

The fields here have a smell, or it's not the smell so much as the texture of the air. The way it enters my lungs. It communicates something to my body. How devastating it is to feel at home when you know it's a fantasy. The body makes its own fantasy out of the sensory input.

While Thomas was mowing his lawn, I went for a walk across the fields. I just kept walking. After a while, I realized where I was walking. When I got there, strangely my first reaction was: What a great house, why would anyone ever sell such a house? I felt like it would be a good investment. Capitalism has infiltrated my nostalgia.

Can there ever be such a thing as "pornography of home"? I mean staring at the place where you're actually from. I didn't want to go inside. I wanted to take away its soul. I can't return. That's what made me feel like I was both drowning and too light to walk. Thomas figured out where I had gone and pulled up in his car, took me back through the fields and fields and they surrounded us.

I want to take away all my ties to this place.

DAY 10

There are so few traces left of the fact that *The Sugar Book* started out as a detective novel. It had the most American plot I could think of: the former starlet (after years of de-bauchery, obscurity, secret films) has been killed. Now it's a headless allegory. A summer book about cake. An overripe summer: bodies are everywhere. I want to count every ant on the cake. It claims to be about Los Angeles but it's really about meadows and poisons.

Is *The Sacrifice* a movie about/in an atmosphere that cannot be cleared, not even by nuclear war? The atmosphere is thick: nature is green, soaking, filmic. The people move in a way that seems both spontaneous and orchestrated (like Woodman's self-portraits). The sounds are too loud: whether footsteps in a distance, the china quivering or the horrifying sound of fighter jets, a booming sound that seems to tear the film itself in half. This is criminal art, art that fails to be moral, despite its religious framing. The atmosphere—like the radiation—contaminates the allegory. In the end we want to give in to madness, become artists, become homeless.

Of course he has to fuck the witch.

This is how art casts its spell—pornographically.

Went into town with Thomas and walked around. Had an ice cream and sat on the benches on Stortorget. Nothing has changed. It was sunny in that dusty way that smells of lilacs. To write *The Sugar Book* I have to become a tourist in my own home. I have to fake my own death. Disappear in order to live here again.

When I was a child my family always went to "Stranden" ("the beach") in the summer. We had a summer house near the coast of the Baltic, where we would spend all day on the beach. The water was always cold and all along the beach there were bunkers left over from World War II where we would play. Once I when I was sitting on the bunker I was burned by a bumblebee. My friend Magdalena told me that bumblebees don't sting, they burn. Another time she held a jellyfish in the palm of her hand and told me jellyfish don't sting in the palm of the hand. She also told me about The Beatles (she loved Ringo but preferred the late Beatles even as a child). Her dad was a journalist like mine, though he did cultural news while my dad reported from Eastern Europe. We would see them every summer. Like me she had a brother, Mathias. He wanted to be a filmmaker. We talked about Hitchcock: our dads, the children. One summer, I think we watched every single Hitchcock movie and TV show on the Swedish Television (the one that left the deepest impression on me was the one about the snake in the pajamas). If the Internet can be believed, Mathias makes reality tv shows now and I write poetry now. I don't know what Magdalena does. I haven't talked to them in 30 years. The people I knew growing up: It makes me furious that they have gone on with their lives, as if I didn't matter at all. I'm still here with the rotten swans.

Tomorrow I move into the apartment in Malmö. I don't know many people in Malmö other than my aunt, Sten and Sara. And I don't actually know Sara, I've just talked to her over email. I know Kristian a little over email as well. I hate being lonely.

I have to make this book into a riddle.
I have to throw away the key.

DAY 11

In essays about "World Literature" critics inevitably bring up the fear of becoming a "tourist." The antidote to this fear is inevitably in these books to learn the original language of the text. Mastery of the original language cures us of anxiety about tourism. Mastery legitimizes our encounter with the foreign text. Mastery means we are not vulnerable to art's ravishing images. In Korea every poem permeated me because I was a tourist.

In Paul Celan's "Paris Memories," the tourists can't breathe until they die.

The Sacrifice is a vacation movie, a tourist film. It could be read autobiographically. Tarkovsky is on vacation in Bergman's Sweden when the Soviet Union returns with a nuclear attack—return of the repressed—to tear apart the fabric of his new life. Tarkovsky had of course abandoned his family in the Soviet Union in order to dedicate himself to his melancholic madness, his art. But Sweden is contaminated by his Russian nostalgia. It's like his nostalgia brings about the end of the world.

The apartment I rent in Malmö has a beautiful terrace but it smells like sperm.

DAY 12

Almost as soon as I got to Malmö yesterday, I left my apartment and went to a library around the corner where Kristian was showing a film about Ernesto Sabado, an author who was involved in the persecution of the military junta in Argentina. The movie was partly a documentary and partly scenes recreated with a surreal dream dramaturgy. Or at least I think it was. Jetlagged, I drifted in and out of sleep. The secret police show up with damaged bodies. Sabado runs on a train looking through documents stored in each train room. A nurse is carrying me down a silent hospital corridor like in 4th grade. I'm watching a play about the Paris Commune with Mathias and Magdalena. Contrary to the common argument that an audience falling asleep is the worst criticism possible against a film, I love falling asleep while watching movies. Some of the best movies I've ever watched were movies I fell asleep while watching. Afterwards I went out with Sten. Then I came home and wrote until early morning.

Everyone in Sweden is talking about Lars Norén's diaries, the second installment of which were just published. Most reviewers are negative. In *Aftonbladet*, Göran Greider manages to accuse Norén of all my favorite charges: Norén is like a spectator in a "spectator democracy"; he's like an Internet troll; if Norén was the head of a country, he'd be a merciless "despot," annihilating cities at random; he's like a mirror; he writes "a kind of pornography for the middle class"; he's "like an animal waiting to be dissected"; and, of course, dead, a corpse. But on the other hands, Greider acknowledges: "when he doesn't hate, his language is the most beautiful I know." Somehow "the most beautiful" can so easily turn into dictatorships, bleeding corpses, animals. Kitsch and its deathy force is all over Greider's thinking. He might as well have called Norén "debased Romanticism."

Could it be that Greider's marxist aesthetics of "simplicity" runs against Norén's often maximalist sensibility? Could it be that his review is an anti-kitsch manifesto? In Norén's books from the 1960s and 70s, there's a feeling like we are entering those beautiful ruins of Tarkovsky's *Stalker*. Ravishing images. Ruin porn.

I haven't seen any of Norén's plays. It's Norén's poetry that matters to me. When I sit down to write, I often imagine that I'm rewriting his book *Revolver* from memory. I need to enter into its atmosphere of an old, collapsing buildings where a woman stands by the big window. The snow is coming in from the ceiling. Maybe the woman by the window is Francesca Woodman. Maybe it's her photographs I write about.

Music about sharp objects. A cutter's music: I'm imagining that I'm writing this in a hospital. I'm always picturing myself in hospitals when I write.

I got an email from Sara. She wanted me to meet the head of Teater Mutation. The three of us met on the square. Went to a bar. They were both younger than me. Sara asked how old I was. I told her. She said I looked younger. The director wore beautiful stockings. Intricate flowers snaking around her legs. Sara brought her child, Kurt, in a baby carriage. We sat outside the bar with him and talked until it started to rain. We talked about fathers who lock up their children, their daughters. That's the subject of the new production Teater Mutation is presenting, *Cleveland*. I asked her if I could sit in on rehearsals. She said she would ask the actresses. When I got back to the apartment I started to write my own captivity narrative, giving the main character a son he keeps in a separate room. I think about Herzog's *Every Man for Himself and God Against All*. Kaspar Hauser. The way he banged that wooden horse against the wall. No not banged. Banged sounds metallic. This was pure wood against stone. More nuanced than banged. Wrote about a Kaspar Hauser situation. But not done out of cruelty exactly. Done to maintain the boy's purity. Which then turns into torture. Everything that America touches turns into torture. I'm an American. Later at night I met up with Sara again. Different bar. Talked until late. She lent me her copy of Norén's diaries. A big black brick. Like a minimalist work of art and/or a gravemarker.

DAY 14

Dreamt of our old home last night. Dreamt there were stitches in my limbs and I didn't want them to come apart. I didn't want to come apart. The damage was from some animal with a difficult neurological illness. My daughters were sitting on the floor sewing something. Somehow I knew that something had to do with death. It became clear to me while watching TV. A show about hares in winter. The blood stained the snow. My mom said the phone call was for me. It was K. who shot himself through the head one winter day in high school. *America.*

Felt sleepy all day. Thought about Bellmer's dolls and the aesthetics of crime photography. Thought about the connection between flowers and luxury. Luxury and sugar. Thought about sugar's history in colonialism. Thought about the metaphor of "spicing up" writing (with metaphors etc). Thought about the role of the exotic in art. Thought about Jack Smith's use of the exotic.

Why am I trying so hard to sound like a teenage girl in these poems?

Because when I use that voice, I am at my most corrupt.

I think about Hawthorne's brilliant murder story "Rappac-cini's Daughter": Raised in the lethal garden, the daughter is exposed to so much poison that she becomes immune to the poison, but it also makes her poisonous. I think it's an allegory about Art. I'm writing a poison book about Amer-ica: Foxglove, hemlock, thousandbeauties.

The Rappaccini's Daughter Complex: I write with poisons. I expose myself to their harm. It's how I stay alive in here. It's why I've returned to the garden.

Thought about Woodman's Mary Janes. Aren't they the same shoes that Hans Bellmer's Doll wears? Googled both of them. Looked at the pictures for 15 minutes. Took out a knife from the kitchen drawer. Put it back in. Wrote a poem about knives that stab through landscape paintings. The Anti-Orpheus Complex is inherently cinematic. I think of myself as something that both permeates and is permeated.

Joyelle wrote. Majken is babbling compulsively. The com-pulsion must be the pleasure of language. Something akin to vandalism. Language scratched the public sphere. The origins of expression is obscenity. My daughter is obscene in her language. Children are obscene. Poetry is obscene. But there are those who want to maintain the illusion that it is good for us.

The Small Traitor of Morality: If I ever write a children's book, that's what I'll call it. The pages stuck together with chewing gum.

My hands are also a key feature of this poem. They seem to want something for me. My wormy little hands. Want me to decorate them as if they belonged to Los Angeles. As if they were losangelessoft and had a motherofpearl sheen. They want me to write about the cold war while they are wrapped in plastic. I think about them like dioramas. I think about them covered with liquid sugar. Sugar doesn't melt, it burns. The dioramas can't last. It's the key to understanding my body: dioramas can't last. The sugar burns holes in them. The ants are everywhere in this apartment. Or my eyes are getting that thing again where I see things crawling all over. *The Crawl* they might have called it in 19th-century Paris. *The Sugar Book* is what I call it in the 21st.

All the lawns are on fire, and all the hands.

I keep thinking about the reading in Copenhagen. The audience included older folks who had come for poetry, jazz (apparently the drummer is the most acclaimed jazz drummer in Denmark) and edification. They liked the other readers. They applauded, chuckled, looked contemplative. When it was my time I couldn't read *Haute Surveillance*. It would have ruined everyone's night. It would have been like taking a shit on the birthday cake. So I read some poems in translation—by Tytti Heikkinen and Kim Hyesoon—but even with these I failed because I started to laugh and had a hard time even reading the words. I don't want to read to an audience that doesn't know my work. Why would I subject them to that? Why would I subject my poems to them?

I should have read my poems. It's exactly the people whose evenings would be ruined by my poems who should have been forced to hear me read them in my ridiculous voice. I should have been torn apart.

When I read everyone should wear rubber gloves.

DAY 15

Reading Sara's copy of Norén's diary. I'm surprised to discover how much of it consists of shopping lists. Like a caricature of the bourgeoisie, he keeps buying fancy clothing, it seems so that he will be forced to remain incredibly productive, writing as many as three plays at the same time. It's as if he's using debt as a kind of currency, a kind of meaning, a reason to keep writing plays.

When did I first meet Sara? When she rewrote my poems from *Pilot* in *Ett lysande namn* as one of her "automanias" (part automatic writing, part mania). How different this is from the kind of appropriative work so common in US experimentalism: Rather than dull and cold, she infuses the text with her own shames and erotics. She wrote: "I am an underage admiresse, an underage fan, of this disease, this contagion." Writing as a kind of contagion, something we make ourselves vulnerable to. Rappaccini's daughter art.

She grasped the shame-saturated, locked-up-ness of the text and didn't just analyze but inserted herself into the text. It seems like this is what Friedlander wants to do with Nazism: to make himself vulnerable to it. But unlike Sara, he can't quite bring himself to fully be taken over. Instructively, his understanding of his texts never reach Sara's understanding of my poems precisely because he doesn't fully give himself to these texts. She gives herself to the texts, becomes poisonous with them.

All this imagery that is coming to me—rubber gloves, mirrors, torn-up Orpheus, Hadean parties—for some reason keep reminding me of the Abu Ghraib photographs. Zizek said somewhere that those photographs documented Iraq's introduction to violent US culture. A kind of hazing, induction. So here I am, having left the US, dreaming its overloaded iconography. Dreaming of Orpheus. Not clear if I'm leaving hell or entering it. Or going from one hell to the next. Poetry belongs in the underworld. Last night I dreamt of an image of Joyelle, scraping a piece of coral with a Swiss Army Knife. All the flakes she gathered into ampules. She was making some sort of medicine. It was for me. An antidote.

DAY 16

I'm writing poems about being a father. That was true also of *Haute Surveillance*. Those weird dreams I still have where Sinead gets somehow pregnant. Those dreams disturbed me. The children are in this book too, but force behind this book is the lethal world they're entering when they leave our house, our Rappacini's garden.

Sometimes when I'm writing poems I find that I'm humming that Nirvana song: "Beat me out of me." That has to do with being Rappaccini's daughter.

It is indicative that most of Friedlander's examples are from the movies: Is this a book about Nazism or a book about the masochistic experience of watching movies? I think of Steven Shaviro's *The Cinematic Body* which argues precisely in favor of "fascination" and against the fearful critics of the movies who argue that this fascination is immoral: "Visual fascination is a passive, irresistible compulsion, and not an assertion of the active mastery of the gaze." Shaviro calls this approach to art masochistic: "The masochism of the cinematic body is rather a passion of disequilibrium and disappropriation. It is dangerous to, and cannot remain the property of, a fixed self. The agitated body multiplies its affects and excitations to the point of sensory overload, pushing itself to its limits... its own transmutation."[2] The danger that Friedlander sees in the "Nazi" aesthetic with its kitsch, death and "ravishing images."

Doesn't Freidlander take the phrase "ravishing images" from Sontag's writing on Leni Riefenstahl's Nazi photographs? Whether she's writing about Nazi photography or pornographic literature, Sontag's very concept of art is shaped by the intersection of art, violence and sexuality. At the end of "Against Interpretation" she famously writes: "In place of a hermeneutics, we need an erotics of art." It sounds like a wish. But a few years later she condemns the "ravishing images" of photography. Later, in *On Regarding the Pain of Others*, she writes: "It seems that the appetite for pictures showing bodies in pain is as keen, almost as the desire for ones that show bodies naked." Sontag longs for a bodily—even erotic— reading of art, but she also fears the imbalanced, unintellectual, graphic result of such a view of art. Pornography names this impossible interaction between body and art.

Beneath a lot of Sontag's judgments is an antagonism against the tourist: a person alienated from surroundings, a person without mastery, a person who doesn't belong. In *On Photography,* Sontag argues that photography has led people in the West to have a "chronic voyeuristic relation" to the world. In *The Pain of Others*, she writes, "The photographer is a supertourist." Voyeurism is of course the realm of the alienated, the foreigner—and it must be condemned as unethical.

---

[2] *Cinematic Body*

Perhaps the origin of the animosity toward "ruin porn" goes back to photography itself, even art itself. At the heart of art is the twin fear of pornography and tourism. Art is always both too distanced and too physically overwhelming. Art is already an erotics.

DAY 17

I think about Sontag's indictment of Diane Arbus: "Arbus's photographs suggest a world in which everybody is an alien." She condemned Arbus for not making the "freaks" sympathetic. But why should we sympathize with the foreign—if by sympathize we really mean to remove the foreignness of that figure? To assimilate them. When people praise works of art for eliciting sympathy or offering situation they can "relate to," what they mean is that the art offers what they already know. It doesn't challenge them. It's not strange.

Sontag charges that Arbus's work came out of "a desire to violate her own innocence."

What is the gurlesque? Maybe: the violation of innocence.

Thinking about the big baby in Stanislav Lem's version of *Solaris*. Thinking about the baby in Aase Berg's *Forsla fett*. Her book is a remake of *Solaris*: but the spaceship has been removed. Thinking about the way the conventional interiority/exteriority divide has been eliminated: the fat is infiltrated by foreign voices, words (those weird words from string theory). Like the fat, the words have no essence: they are mistranslations, perversions. They are "fat." Not communication but the transfer of fat.

The sugar is leading to an all-out assault: "god against all." The violence is like an atmospheric violence, a plague that strikes everyone: Bodies strewn everywhere.

Bought Eva-Kristina Olsson's new book *Eiderwhite*. She doesn't give a shit about "accessible" or "sincere." Language melts and is reshaped in her poems. If ornament is a crime, she foregrounds the ornamentation of the crime scene. She brings artifice out of anatomies and make jewelry anatomical.

There's something operatic about wearing a Reagan mask made of rubber. Whether you fuck with it on your head or rob a bank with it on your head or beg for coins with it on your head it's transformative. The name Reagan marks my transition into adulthood. A counterfeiter determined my life. A cold war shaped my art. I write as if poetry was another name for Berlin. The walls are still standing.

Reading *The Parapornographic Manifesto*, by Carl-Michael Edenborg. Edenborg argues that there is an "illusion on which both pornography and anti-pornograpy rest" and that's that "beauty hides a shameful secret." Pornography and anti-pornography share a basic worldview. Against this, Edenborg argues for a parapornography that rejects this binary without erasing the stuff of porn. The US literary gatekeepers are neither pro, anti or parapornography. They want to create the illusion that there is no porn. There are no clothes beneath which they "access" the point of the poem; the clothes do not cover up, nor do they eroticize. During the Ann Jäderlund Debates, one reviewer objected to Jäderlund's poems flirting with him but failing to fully reveal her feelings. He wanted simplicity, accessibility. She gave him keyholes through which to peek, through which to have his eyes gouged.

The rhetoric of masks is everywhere in US poetry discussions: elitist critics tell us we need to avoid masks, write "accessible" poetry; there's that famous 1970s anthology of feminist poetry, *No More Masks*. Both posits an authentic interior that is then covered over by masks. But masks can be carnivalesque. Think about Zurita posing as a female prostitute in an act of resistance to Pinochet's dictatorship. Masks can be political. Masks can reek of sweat, like my Olsson-mask. It's made from duck feathers.

DAY 18

Woke up with the phrase "You can call me Crime Flower this autumn" playing in my head. Thought about that time the kid at LSU was arrested when someone thought his imitations of my poems meant that he was about to shoot the school up. Crime of art, art of crime.

What is this thief's journal I'm writing? I have to erase these pieces from *The Sugar Book*. They don't belong. I don't want my life to ruin the book. I want to leave that to the inmates. It's their book. I'm just building the stage so that they can tear it down. Their voices are circulating through my head. More corpses for poetry.

I saw a landscape painting torn by a dull knife. Saw a tree that looked like it consisted of tangled limbs. I was out walking. Stopped by the People's Park. Thought about the riot. Thought about the paintings of the riot. Saw a horse-slaughter. It was the Paris Commune. The sentence about Crime Flower was its voice over.

Gertrude Stein supposedly said she went to France to be alone with the English language. I went back to Sweden to be contaminated by Swedish.

Thought about Mathias and Magdalena. I emailed their father and he sent me their phone numbers. Of course the problem persists: they have moved on and lived entire lives without me. I have never been able to. I'm stalking them in my own rat-infested memory mansion.

Saw the horrible photographs of refugees lined up in a harbor. Sometimes art fails. Art has to fail, how could they succeed in a world like this? All those "ravishing images" of the corpses: I hope they violate any innocence that is left in this horrible world. No more innocence. No more Quietist poems to make us feel good about being human. The stage has to be torn down. Not violence as purifying but destruction as complicating. Violence isn't clean. Poetry isn't clean. I'm taking down what the voices tell me.

"To cut forth the essential" (Sept 2000): From the beginning of Norén's diary there's an emphasis on "simplicity" and "cleanliness." He's constantly cleaning his apartment. And in his writing, he "skriver rent" [literally "writes clean"] his plays—as if revising was a matter of cleaning them up. It's a rhetoric of abjection. While cleaning his apartment, he writes that he is "sorting" out the junk from the stuff he wants to save. If he's "sorting out" his writing, what are the parts he wants to keep and what are the parts he want to get rid of? Or is the diary the ultimately "clean" text: I do this, I do that. The sentences are short, often he writes without any transitions. Diary as montage of curt sentences. He wants to clean by writing, but writing produces art, ie filth.

Norén sorting his apartment: ground zero for art's impossibility. Me sitting in room that smells like sperm writing about Los Angeles: ground zero for homesickness.

Went out in the evening. Met Sten at Folkets Park. It's been shut down for the reason. Some teenagers with bicycles were fucking around with an abandoned shed and I couldn't see Sten at first because he was hiding from the teenagers. Quickly appeared and drew me away from them. Never occurred to me to be scared of them. Does that mean I'm stupid?

DAY 19

Children are obscene.

Today I wish I could hear my own children's prattling.

Since becoming a father I've become so sentimental. There's nothing as horrifying as violence against children. I've become a version of the Kaspar Hauser father: I want to lock up my daughters so that nothing will ever happen to them. It's impossible to be a father. I'm an impossible father.

Had a dream last night. Joyelle was giving me head but she was also Maria Nilsson and we were teenagers and my parents were home and my cock was shaped like one of those double-popsicles we used to eat as kids. The flavor was coca-cola.

Thinking about the movie about Keats. The butterflies are supposed to represent Art. But they also stand in for sex. I'm writing teenage poetry: sex and butterflies. Every anatomy has to be wounded.

Norén is pissed at a critic for calling *7:3* a "peepshow." Since it's a play that consists—from what I can tell—primarily of people sitting around in a room discussing Nazism, I have to conclude that Nazism is a naked body (or a body with just a little bit of undergarment). In his *Parapornographic Manifesto*, Carl-Michael argues against the pornographic concept that depends on an interiority that can be revealed. I think about all those Swedish detective shows where Nazism is the dirty secret that has to be revealed. Nazism it seems proves that the country has an interiority. Perhaps Norén thinks the same way: that only by curing the secret, Nazism, he can cure the country.

I think I can't cure the English language but I can poison it with flowers. The conventional way of viewing language as a kernel of meaning that has to be grasped is fundamentally pornographic. This is why any texts or aesthetics that suggest the noise of that operation, its ultimate illusoriness, has to be condemned as pornography. Sensational: I write in a contaminated language.

This must be why I'm writing in a kind of imaginary teenage slang—a language made out of and for contamination. A language with holes in it. I'm not imitating real slang. I'm making it talk with the end of the world and all of its contagions and butcheries. It's like, anybody wearing a Reagan mask can fuck me because I love operas. I'm cutting them up in an homage to the mall.

I have gotten into a rhythm. I know when the sadness will strike. When I have to start walking.

Today I walked around for hours as if searching for something. Wasn't searching for anything. Was searching for an entrance, a hole through which I could come home. I found the portal briefly. It was a tree on the edge of People's Park that seemed to shudder in the wind. It said something to me. It had small leaves. Was it an elm tree? I used to know the names of all trees, shrubs, berries, mushrooms. Now they're just trees, shrubs, berries, mushrooms. This is what the tree said to me. It said you're a number.

I walk and I remember and I expect to see someone I know but I don't. I love it when people say they "belong" somewhere. Maybe because the place overwhelms individual agency. Maybe because I belong to summer. I belong to a poem about summer. Written by Eva Kristina Olsson. A ghost story about home.

DAY 20

Dreamt I followed the sperm odor around the apartment trying to find the source of it. I followed it into the closet which lead to another room that I hadn't known about. The room was empty except for three figurines. "The Virgin Sisters." At first the figurines seemed tiny, maybe the size of my pinkie, but when I held them they seemed much larger, the size of small dogs. Those rat-like dogs. Whatever they are called. It turned out the war had begun. I could hear the airplanes. This room was my shelter. It was the three sisters that were emanating the sperm odor. I tried to wipe them off with my sleeve but nothing helped. They looked glossy at first. Then I realized that everything in this room, including my hands, had a certain luster. The kind of luster caused by an intense fever.

I wrote poems about the riddles of Woodman, about the riddle that pornography posits: we have to tear the clothes off, then we have to tear the skin off. We have to scratch a message on the poem's heart with bird claws. I wrote a poem about a "Chinese bed." It's hard to believe how many poems I'm writing, but this book has a force that generates itself. I am almost just listening. The dead tell me anything I write becomes poetry. So I write anything. It's a kind of debased mall-orphism: foxglove, hemlock, iron weed.

Suddenly memories from years ago came back to me: the shooting range. I thought about A. How strong she was when she held me down.

Have been having trouble with my eyesight again. Keep seeing things that are not there. Insects mostly but also figures that trail off. I hate bubble gum but I want more bubble gum in the poem. And I'm thinking about anorexia again. And loud sounds. What they do to the texture of the poem. And about torsos. The vulnerability of torsos. Thought about the box as a unit of composition. Thought about arranging the objects in the box. Thought about dioramas. Thought about why I associate my arms with dioramas. Thought about Plath's bees. Thought about the color red. Thought I would invent a new dance craze. Then I saw some more insects on the pages of the book. Maybe this is what they used to call visions. Something is fucked up with one's eyes and it's a sign. I see insects on my book because it's a sugar book.

In Eva Kristina Olsson's *Eiderwhite*, it's the snailish, mother-of-pearl moisture that captivates me. Like a gross horror movie transformation elevated to a grotesque spirituality. This is what's so lacking in all these epiphanies of literature: the violence and grossness of being transformed, changed. This is what's lacking in all these works "embracing the body": its beauty is disgusting.

The blood-smeared handprint on the *Eiderwhite* cover seems evidence of a violent crime, but it could also be ink smears. The crime of writing: it makes art out of one's body, one's hands.

The torture imagery that I associate with Cocteau's *Orpheus* —doesn't it also come from Chris Marker's *La Jetée*? They try to torture the main character into remembering his past, his home, which has been destroyed by World War III. The capacity to remember—homesickness, nostalgia—also allows him to travel forward in time, to imagine a brilliant future. The movie thus dispels the common assumption that we must leave our pasts behind in order to progress. We will only survive through melancholy. We won't survive.

Met up with Sten last night. He told me about writing his books on that Zen Buddhist guru he keeps following around. Explained how he had started to doubt his transcription methods. He had been faithfully writing down whatever the guru told him, but then he decided that there was too much noise in this process. His memory was simply not strong enough. So he started carrying a recorder around with him to get every single word down. After a while of transcribing these recordings, he realized that not only might his translation skills be flawed, he was communicating with the guru in English, the guru's second language. And then he became nervous that he wasn't capturing all the pauses, the hemming and hawing that suddenly seemed so important to the guru's way of speaking. When he had finally completed all the transcription in a satisfactory way, he realized that there were other voices in the recordings, the voices of other Zen Buddhists who had participated in retreats, attended lectures etc. When he asked them if it was OK for him to use them in his book, they were furious, demanding that he withdraw their names, and, when he had done that, demanding that he add misleading information about them so that nobody would guess it was them. For example, one man wanted to be identified as a Christian woman from Germany.

The masquerade as a form of legal protection: the use of masks destabilizes all identities. I'm wearing a mask in *The Sugar Book*. A torn-up rubber Orpheus mask made by Richard Hawkins in LA.

Norén says he gets melancholy when he buys beautiful clothes because he knows that he's going to die and then he will no longer be able to wear them. I get melancholy in front of the mirror because I am in front of a mirror: I can see myself. I really can. I'm there.

People ask me why I don't write in Swedish. I always write in Swedish.

DAY 21

Dreamt of an image of myself. A photograph I couldn't really make out but I knew it was of me. The lamp created a glare. And the woman who held the lamp: her other hand was on my shoulder. She had the vague fragrance of grass about her. She said she took it the last time I was home. When was that I asked. I was always scared as a child.

If the second half of the crime book is the genre's enforced redemption of the over-the-top sensationalistic first half with its crime scenes and mysterious corpses. What happens if one keeps going without the redemption? One writes something truly glamorous and evil.

I love stunt doubles the same way I love painters.

I think about the stunt double in Ballard's *Crash*. How leaving the central drama seems to push him into an ever-widening orbit of volatility: he becomes an impersonator of death-bound Jayne Mansfield, driving in the outskirts of the novel, a volatile agent of disruption that cannot quite even be brought into the narrative of the novel, or of Vaughn's planned assassination attempt on Liz Taylor. This is a headless allegory—physical, sensational, fatal—about the glamour of poetry. What I appreciate about this death-drive is his focus. To veer away from the plot—with its motives and characters—does not mean to become aimless, but perhaps to become even more focused, faster, more intoxicated. The goal: to become photographed as a corpse. To be Blanchot's image.

Everything is always already mass produced because it's seen through the lens of a camera. Vaughn is a purveyor of kitsch, not unlike Andy Warhol. The difference is of course that Warhol is entirely desexualizing in his reproductions, while Vaughn is desperately hypersexual, a pornographer. The key to the sexuality—which the novels at times appears to condemn—is that it's a stand in for art: how art transgresses our boundaries of selfhood. It makes wounds in us.

We make meadows to trick ourselves that we are home, back in time, before artifice, commerce, movement, industry. In Jäderlund the meadow is its own contamination. Beautiful. Cut up. The violence is in the meadow. Just like those songs we used to sing in church on the last day of school. Threatening songs about flowers. I'm also writing a cutter's book. I'm also strewing the flowers throughout Los Angeles like corpses. Grainy images, smeared street scenes: There's no music in my book. Just a drone, a hum, like we are underwater.

Pildamsparken is unnaturally green, flowers still blooming even though it's fall. People lounged on the lawn. When I walked through a kind of corridor of trees, someone else walked along with me, outside the trees. But he wasn't there when I reached the end. He had left me a message: a desiccated bird. Do I know you, I asked nobody at all. It was not even evening when I began to drink in this room that still smells like sperm. The flowers in this apartment are tropical, there's a fat glow in the leaves that goes with the sperm and the man in the park, who carried something similar on his back. At first I thought it was a child but now I think it must have been a poisonous flower.

DAY 22

The melancholic always goes back, can't stop going back, lives in the past, the past saturating their lives. The melancholic is unproductive. The melancholic is something akin to the traditional figure of the masturbator. There's something not just unhealthy but fake about them. They have to become poets or suicides.

I hate it when people dimiss certain poems as "masturbative" because I think those are often the best texts, texts that dare to not try to "communicate" and instead can open up a zone where the writer's childish fascinations can lead the way. Language loses its transparency. It's no longer based on reporting interiority but on fantasizing. The stalker in Tarkovsky's movie is seen as perverse, pathological. A masturbator of sorts.

I'm thinking about Stina Kajaso. *Wosh wosh blood tsunami*. I want to go all butchered deer in the collage machine. All porno with toy gun in a bunny costume. I'm writing *The Sugar Book* under her toxic influence. Influence is so much more interesting when it comes from the margins than when it comes from the Greats. On Solaris, we cut up teenage celebrity magazines. Wosh wosh. Everybody is pornographic in this costume. In this costume I become nostalgic for my own death. The one that took place years ago, on the front lawn. I wrote a poem about it once and dedicated it to my widows. Widow Party.

I'm writing about a shitty Orpheus: "My wife tells me that the road to joy is littered// with corpses. I think they have sperm on them.///She thinks they have Xs on them."

Orpheus is a figure of inflation: he is torn into pieces.

I'm writing about a plague that is killing teenage girls in droves. Is it the teenage language that is killing them, killing me. No it's something horrific—like radiation—working on us all invisibly. At first I wrote about a dictatorial governor, but it doesn't seem right. I'm removing him. The murders and contaminations are working invisibly. The guards at Abu Ghraib were bad apples following an invisible but highly aesthetic order. The Order of the Rubber Gloves. We are contaminated.

I ask Sara what she thinks of Francesca Woodman.

She says: "I think the cliché is right. All those critics and curators wanted to fuck her."

Do they want to fuck her or do they want to be fucked by her. Whose innocence is violated here? Woodman brings out the "erotics" of art but she makes a homelessness for the viewer. She makes a wound in me. Perhaps she is a kind of ruin pornographer after all.

My poems are written like shells that accumulate. They are disgusting because they are also flowers: Foxglove, thousand-beauties, corpse flowers, priest collars. They are disgusting because the translations keep failing. Are failed translations pornographic because they foreground their own version-ness. I'm not at home in poems.

DAY 23

Wrote for four hours on *The Sugar Book* today. Wrote an answer to the tree in People's Park. I began by trying to tell it why I wanted to go home. But I had to do it in the tree's language. The twitchy, flickering language it had used when it told me about my ignorance. In another age, it would have told me about heaven.

Thought about the man in the park and the desiccated bird. How do I know it was even a man. The figure's rhythm was so finely attuned to mine it was like it moved behind a tree every moment I moved clear of them. Began to wonder if I had created this figure. If I had placed that strange object on its back because I wanted it to suffer. When I came back I began to make elaborate plans for my torso. In Los Angeles there must be many dummies.

Thought again about the death-row section of the book. Erased it. Put it back in. The text must destroy itself. Me. So I erased it. So I put it back. Instead I erased the part about Michael Jackson and torture porn. Erased the part about Bellmer and the shoes. Thought about "Son of Daddy." Thought about Sara's wounding and wounded theatricality. Thought about the gaze. Thought about Bellmer's crime photos of tied-up Zürn. Thought about US literature's anxiety about theatricality. Thought I should rename *The Sugar Book* as *Why Are You Doing This To Me?* Thought about renaming it *The Pornography* as an act of shame. Walked to the pizzeria. Became depressed while waiting for my pizza. I put the voices back in. All of them. I put them back in. I'm making the text eat itself. It's full of shame.

Later I walked again. Thought about the vermin metaphor. Thought about the leftist tendency to valorize home, natural relations. The foreigner ruins the community. But humanity is obviously parasites. I'm obviously a parasite. I'm trying to find my home. But all I find is the excess. Walked. Tried to find the tree again. Couldn't. Emailed Sara. Emailed Sten. Printed out a copy of Reagan's face. Made a mask. Took a photograph of myself in the People's Park in front of another tree. It was the wrong tree, the wrong face. Later drank with Sara. She bought cigarettes at "Baghdad livs." There was a photograph of a park behind the clerk. I asked him what it was. He said that it was in Baghdad. He said he used to live in Baghdad.

DAY 24

Dreamt about Medea's tree on fire, her children like lanterns rocking on the branches. I wanted to extinguish the lanterns but when I got close enough to put out the fires I found that the lanterns were small flowers, the size of eggs, the folds intricate. The fire came from inside the flowers.

Publisher's Weekly has reviewed *Haute Surveillance*, calling it "pornography" and akin to "channel surfing." The anonymous critic writes: "Göransson's celebratory and orgiastic barrage of smut reiterates an already exhausted critique of political theater, nihilistic spectatorship, and American popular culture. The shock of this screed is undermined by sheer unrelenting volume making for a cringe-inducing text that feels paradoxically abrasive and cliché. What Görannson has created is a vacuous form of post-modernism that feels more like an exercise in masochism than boundary-pushing experimentation."

So what I write is pornography, but I have also somehow managed to turn it into "critique." It is a perceptive review, capturing the "cringe-inducing" and "unrelenting" quality of the book, but for some reason the critic can't understand that I don't hate "nihilistic spectatorship." The critic is perceptive but can't follow the book where it takes them: they seem to be overwhelmed by the need to condemn the book.

Why masochism and not sadism?

Have they ever read *Crash* or *Our Lady of Flowers*?

Behind the *PW*'s critic's objection is a somewhat strange assumption: My book is bad because it's pornographic, but also because in its "unrelenting volume," it fails to be good pornography. I'm sorry you couldn't get off on my book, *Publisher's Weekly*. The foreigner makes porn, but the foreigner fails. The result: kitsch, inflation.

The Sugar Book has to be more pornographic, has to have more sugar in it—or rather on it. Sugar is always on the surface: glistening, burning or powdering the skin. The movement associated with sugar is spasmodic. It might tear a whole in the fabric, the skin. Burn a hole. This is where the atmosphere leaks in. And it's the atmosphere more than anything else that cannot be redeemed. Art as crime. Art as convulsive surface. If art doesn't have "depth" it has to have cuts.

I think about Daniel Tiffany's work on kitsch, his quote of Herman Broch: "Kitsch is a foreign body lodged in the overall system of art." *Publishers Weekly* is the "industry standard," mean to protect the American "system" from foreign bodies—tasteless and tastelessly embodied. "Gatekeepers" like *PW* are so set on defending their supposedly democratic ideal of moderation, which is really a very elitist notion of taste. Kristeva might have said: the foreign bodies are pollutants.

In *The Emancipation of the Spectator*, Ranciere finds the roots of the attacks on the excess and—pornographic?—thrills of mass culture in the old elite's fear of mass culture. Those same people are still running *Publishers Weekly*: trying to maintain a sense of restraint and moderation. The threat is always the sensational—i.e. art that affects the senses, instead of the soul. The "barrage" will damage you. The "morass" will drown you. This is the art we have to be protected against: an art that overwhelms, affects. You will not be in charge.

The excessive language of the review undermines its evaluation: it is this and that and also that. There are too many analogies. The excess of the my book has apparently contaminated the singularity of the reviewer's evaluation. To be a master, you speak more precisely, economically. You cannot give in to the morass of language.

PW's critic is right about the "masochistic" aspect of my book. In Shaviro's *The Cinematic Body*, he argues against film theorists' iconophobia, writing of his own engagement with films: "My own masochistic theoretical inclination is to revel in my bondage to images, to celebrate the spectatorial condition of metaphysical alienation and ideological delusion, rather than strive to rectify it."

Had a great time visiting Leif. The walls of his apartment are covered with shelves and shelves of books and videos and DVDs. And the leftover structures from various art performances. I've only seen Leif's art in photographs, never in life. His work is like conceptual art but bodily and material rather than conceptual, like Joseph Beuys if he had realized the power of kitsch, or a gay Matthew Barney without the million-dollar budget. We talked about Aase and horror movies, outfits that kill, trash as art and art as trash. He used to publish poetry as a woman, Katarina Ytterbom, while making art as a man. Now he just uses his own name but in his art I noticed that he often appears in costumes that hide his face. Often he wears so many clothes they seem to strangle him. A lot of the pieces consists of trash or make trash out of practical objects, like when he saws a sofa in half. One of my favorite pieces is a knitted, pink testicle-warmer dedicated to Matthew Barney. What is trash and art, kitsch and horror is never clear, but it's not at all "unclear," it's more like a clashing, art as a reckoning with material, with the soul, with gender. Luckily he has an installation at the art school down the street from me.

Who am I writing this for? Is this part of *The Sugar Book*? Should I translate it back into Swedish? Is it just fake English? This text can't be translated because it's a counterfeit; it's not an original. A contaminated original is no longer an original, it's a dead swan with ants crawling through the folds of the feathers.

The experience of being a foreigner in one's own home: I keep walking around Malmö expecting to see people I know. I'm going to go see my aunt tomorrow. She lives over in Ribbersberg. "Oh, Ribban. That's where the real Malmö-ites from way back live," says Sara.

Fell asleep early. Woke up an hour later with these words in my head: "I turn on suveillance, turn on heat. / The effect is ominous: the reverse wound./I look horrified in the image and also "satanic" due to the milk./You spumey fuck."

DAY 25

I sent a batch of poems to Joyelle. Joyelle wrote: "Read Nijinisky's diary. He had similar plans to you." I'm starting to think of *The Sugar Book*s as a diary rather than a novel. A nervous diary.

In his diaries, Norén keeps comparing his poetry to an "over-exposed photograph." If his poetry is pornographic, it's the kind of pornography that makes bodies illegible.

Greider calls Norén a pornographer, but it's Greider who wants to smash the mirror, to find the hidden truth. Perhaps the pornographer and the iconoclast are always in cahoots, as Carl Michael suggests. As Blanchot compares the image to a corpse, might we not see Norén as an image-proliferator. Corpse artist.

The humanist aesthetic of simplicity and restraint demands interiority because it's fundamentally an economic world-view: It fears the inflation of words and images. It demands a gold standard: the soul.

Sontag dislikes Arbus because she can't feel sympathy toward Arbus's "freaks." They have no interiority. Arbus violates Sontag's demand for interiority. They proliferate and overwhelm. Sontag drowns in Arbus's morass. Her erotics become pornography, ravishing images.

When I write I feel myself fainting—into what? Into a mirror. But it's not a hard mirror, the mirror doesn't break. It's fluid, but it's not water, it has the consistency of melted metal. I write as I move through it, as it moves through me. This is why they call writing the fainting disease. It's about mediumicity.

My hands have begun to move in a slightly new way. I can't explain it but they move with less certainty, yet with wider scope, especially when I stop by the tree in People's Park. I have to keep my hands in my pockets not to draw attention to them. There's a place on the corner there that I want to enter, they sell "bread." But I don't dare because I fear that my hands' movement would be obscene in there, in that hole in the wall.

Maybe the reason I'm so fascinated by Kaspar Hauser tales is my own irrational fear of letting my daughters out of my sight. The second they turn a corner, I'm wracked with fear. It's like an infant who thinks that if they can't see the object, it doesn't exist. The result is a kind of hoarder urge.

Thought: We should replace all roses with ironweed because it's more beautiful and butterflies love it. Thought: Especially in poetry. Just erase every mention of rose and insert iron-weed, blazing star, goldenrods. Poetry would finally be totally American. Totally enswarmed with butterflies. Like in that sex dream I keep having. Endymion.

Did I write about the man I've been seeing in the corner of my eyes doing strange things, emitting strange sounds? Today I thought: If I'm writing this book like a ghost, and yet this man appears to be a ghost that is haunting me, the one who haunts this original country, then perhaps—via the logic of the double negative—he is the only one who can actually see me. I told this to Sara. She told me about the underground years, the underworld years, the sexuality and the violence. Syringes remind me of roses. I love/hate the image of a syringe but I love the sound of a glass syringe shattering on tiles. The man I see, he has something to do with syringes but also with flowers.

I've been trying to call Magdalena. She doesn't answer. I left a strange message. I didn't know what to say. I've come back 30 years later and I want to know what became of you. Sincerely, a ghost.

In *The Sugar Book*, the detective superimposes photographs of the victim's body on maps of Los Angeles to figure out where to find the killer. He finds it in the heart of course. Except it's not the killer, it's racist state violence. It's an occult star map. In Malmö I follow another map: rotten fruit, my body, words in Swedish pop songs.

DAY 26

This morning, a feeling of utter aftermath. Woke up early and went to the store to buy some breakfast, but it was too early so I walked around the desolate neighborhood. Cities are always most beautiful at 6 am. The light coming on but few people. I saw posters for "Too Cute to Puke" and "Young, Lean, Sad Boys." I've always loved band names. There was also the poster announcing *The Act of Killing*. Then the bikers came and the cars and then the cafe opened and I bought a cup of latte and watched the world take shape. I went to the grocery store and got a bottle of kefir. Raspberry flavored.

To get in the mood to write, I sit by the window and imagine that I'm in a hospital with a bandaged head, that my body is hairless, that the erotics of shards is my subject matter. It's like summer will never end, I read in the kill book.

Notley's *Descent of Alette* both stages the Jungian journey (to pass through the inhuman pornography of the underworld into personhood) and in *staging* it, undermines the journey-narrative. Turns it into performance art. The art wins. We will never leave the underworld, Alice. I don't want to.

I'm writing the book as a performance instruction. Point number six, use a shitty typewriter to type out the voices from deathrow. Point number twelve: go to Korea and hear voices when you look at a squid. Number twenty two: Of course you're naked. Number forty-eight: I want to die in grass. Number sixty-two: The point of dyeing snow with melted candy would be to show that the blood is coming from without. Performance art is always allegory. The body is always threatening to make the vehicle too much for the tenor. The struggle for the conservative artist is to use the allegory to eliminate the pornographic. The underworld is lined with bodies. The road to joy is lined like an allegory.

Went to see Leif's exhibit. Unfortunately the janitors had thought it was trash and thrown it away. Fortunately Leif had managed to save the trash. Sara and her friend read the poems—idealized propositions about the welfare state. I went back to my apartment and now I'm working on *The Sugar Book*. My poems must be trashier, shittier, even more extravagant in their inflationary production.

I wrote about Leif's play in *The Sugar Book* that it was about a kind of self-fucking, self-violating art. I thought of the racist phrase "black-on-black violence" but changed it to "violence-on-violence violence." We might condemn the janitor as a moron, or we might see that he was put under art's spell.

The strange confluence of experimental art and pornography, trash and high art. I think about Kenneth Anger, whose movies were shown in a porn theater in Time Square. I think about Sontag's description of the pornographic that which does not grant interiority to the bodies. How it's similar to the best, most artistic cinema, for example *Faster Pussycat Kill Kill* with its aimless visions of California dustscape.

I hate everyone today. I want to have a silk shirt. I want to set it on fire. Fell asleep. Dreamt about a dancer. Very beautiful. Far more fluid than I had imagined. The dancer wants to be back in the book but I keep erasing him. I asked Joyelle and she said "Don't worry about it, just write." Thought about what she said about the braille-machine. Wanted to write a portrait of a tower on fire with a braille machine.

Many people don't realize that I write not to shock them but because I'm hypersensitive. I'm trying to survive.

Wrote about fruit juices and insects. Wrote about Greek mythology: seed. Walked through the square. Wondered if all the houses would fall down. Walked through the abandoned People's Park. Looked at the orientalist façade. Thought about Bellmer's shoes. About the strange man with the desiccated bird. What kind of language was that bird? Thought about femurs and ankles and adam's apples. Thought about apples on the ground. Bought elderberry drink. Read Eva Kristina Olsson's book with the bloody handprint on the cover.

Drank with Sara. She told me about her production of *'Tis Pity She's a Whore*. I told her about *The Duchess of Malfi* I was in, at the shooting range. I told her about the wax sculptures. The paper sculptures. How they burnt. I told her about gasoline and my skin. She told me about roller skating.

Sara asked why I write so much about prostitutes. Because they are vulnerable, I told her. Because their vulnerability exists at the intersection of private and public. Then I told her how I saw that thing in Atlanta.

I love the word anemone.

Malmö is a city built for exercises in the afterlife. As I walk around, I strike my best Orphée pose.

DAY 27

The reading went well. I read with an Iranian poet named Azita Ghahreman, who read beautiful political poems, and a Japanese expat named Hikaru Sugi. Ghahreman wrote beautifully poetic pieces and gave me a copy of her book (published by Kristian) after the reading. Sugi showed us how to make oragami cranes instead of reading. Kristian read a beautiful excerpt of his translation of Hart Crane's *The Bridge*. It sounded better in Swedish. Sounded like Strunge. So it was strange that afterwards, Clemens Altgård came and introduced himself. I said his translation of Strunge was my first favorite book and we started to talk about Strunge and Burroughs. But I could tell Sara wanted to hang out, so I told him we would meet for coffee today.

The Voice That Is Great Within You: that anthology from the 1970s. What could it say about possessions?

Joyelle writes that she and the children watched a Japanime show where a dog drowns in some kind of thick jelly. Our daughters think the puppy died even though in the movie it came back and saved the day. They are confused and terrified. "I don't know anything about dogs!" she writes.

In a review-interview of Sara's novel *Mumieland* for *Sydsvenska Dagbladet*, the reviewer, Matilda Gustavsson, begins by describing how Sara stages "distorted self-portraits" in Heidi Fleiss's trailer: "she lets her own biography melt together with the bordello mamma: Tuss—Fluss—Fleiss. The shitty glamour of Los Angeles merges with 1990s Falun kicker-chicks, buffaloes and big aquariums." Gustavsson catches the permutative confessionalism of Sara's writing, punning her name together with Fleiss's in a way that also for me invokes the beginning of *Lolita*.

The review focuses on the role of the grotesque, saturated body in the novel. And that is what sticks out in my mind most clearly: the dolls, the mother's sick, oozing body, the whores' consumed bodies, the girl's pubescent body. Sara says one of her main inspirations is "porn": "I am drawn to it the way I'm drawn to gothic novels and wrestling. How the framing and the needs are so exaggerated. That the strong feelings seem mechanical."

It's because porn's mechanical bodies have no souls that Sara's novel melts together with Heidi Fleiss, infects the reviewers' language, makes the language masturbatory. This is the infection of a kind of art I am interested in. This is the inflation that *The Sugar Book* wants to both explore and make itself vulnerable to.

Glad Sontag's famous essay, "The Pornographic Imagination," is online. Here she defends "pornographic" literature—Bataille, Sade etc—from US puritanical critics' general sense that "pornography" is a "malady." They can't understand how something can be "pornographic" and have literary value, so Sontag goes about rescuing this tradition from the charges of malady. Must it be made into "great literature"? Maybe the greatness is that it isn't great. Bataille's *Story of the Eye, Blue of Noon*—they are incomplete, failures as novels. They are also some of the best novels ever written.

Sontag describes one of the main features of pornography as the interchangeability of characters: interiority is not an important part of pornography. Bodies are bodies. Isn't this something like the lack of "human" empathy for which she takes Arbus to task? Is it perhaps that Sontag couldn't recognize Arbus for what she was (a pornographer).

One of Sontag's most interesting points is that pornography does not just have to do with nudity but also formal aesthetics: "Another argument, made by Adorno and others, is that pornography lacks the beginning-middle-end form characteristic of literature. A piece of pornographic fiction concocts no better than a crude excuse for a beginning; and once having begun it goes on and on, and ends nowhere." Pornography has to do with a formal failure of narrative, a failure to get to a sense of completion. This explains why conservative institutions like *Publishers Weekly* treat things that fail to comply with its norms as immoral.

No great work of art was ever tasteful. The lines I'm writing are so sweet, it's like sucking nectar from a bright red corpse flower. Dirty bird, hello.

Thrilled to have found the key move for the entire book. When I cut up the sentences, drain them of their sentence-to-sentence momentum they develop their own sloppy, undead energy. Anything I write goes into the slaughterhouse of language. I was always most of all interested in the unearned line.

DAY 28

Had very interesting meeting with Clemens Altgård. He told me about Malmö in the 80s. How the government and corporations had decided to tear down huge parts of it but that it would be cheaper to just let it collapse on its own. Talked about the freedom of an art scene burgeoning so far from the center, not just from New York or Paris but even from Stockholm, in a town that was collapsing. He told me he thought Norén's diary sounded like Brett Easton Ellis's *American Psycho*. He's right: the flat voice, short sentences, lists of products (including art). We started talking about Bellmer and he gave me a book from the seventies about Bellmer with poems by Norén.

I've moved back to the balcony to write. But I can't help but smell the smell of sperm and it's entering my book on every other page. My book about sugar is becoming a book about sperm.

It strikes me that *The Sugar Book* has become a kind of diary. Everything I write goes in. Nothing feels superfluous. Everything feels both huge and precise. Norén would hate what I write. Maybe I'm writing two books: *The Sugar Book* and Norén's diaries.

Norén is tired and sick a lot. He has diarrhea, headache and gets a jaw infection. His face begins to "look like a painting by Francis Bacon." What's the role of the sick body in this book? Does it ruin the concentration, precision, simplicity? Or does it reduce the text to a simple bodily force? No, it seems to give the text a heightened precision.

Often in contemporary US poetry, people promote writing "the body." But the body is often sick and makes you do stupid shit. The body wants to consume. The body is sick. My skin bubbles up. I'm turning into a monster. I will soon need Leif to make me a beautiful uniform of trash to hide my ugliness.

Today I saw behind a window, partially hidden by the sun's reflection, a man with close-cropped blonde hair and beard. It wasn't me because he had tattoos on his upperarm. I couldn't read what they said. I couldn't see what he was doing there but he appeared to have his head in his hands. He looked like me but he was not the one who has been following me. In fact, I'm the one who's following him. He's in there, in a private space, where I can never be again.

Let me in.

Sara left town today. I was supposed to meet her and give her back her copy of Norén's diary, but I got very tired and messaged her that I was too tired to walk over to her place and she wrote back that it was OK that she was never going to read that book anyway, that I could throw it away. But I can't do that. I'll drag this black grave marker of a book along with me to Göteborg and Stockholm.

DAY 29

In a dream the follower came back to me. Brought with him: prairie flowers. He coated them in gasoline. I had always thought he came from here, but he came from back there, the US. Perhaps he is coming to bring me finally home. The fire isolated me. People were calling from the other side. I couldn't go there. You shouldn't have used that on the angel said the follower and pointed to my right hand which held an elaborate fire iron. Shaped like a gladiolus. I thought it was you, I confessed.

You can never burn your home down says the photographer in a Macedonian movie we watched last night. It was made in the nineties while the Balkan peninsula was burning down. It's about a photographer who returns home from a cosmopolitan life working around world taking exotic photographs for western publications. He goes home, to meet the woman he loved as a young man, to become who he was—not a copy but the original—but when he gets there his home doesn't exist anymore, or rather it's been split in two, Muslims against Christians. He tears up his exotic photographs as if this will allow him to be whole but it has the opposite effect: he gets caught in the fighting and is killed. Killed for trying to return to summer. Maybe a foreigner can only come home through civil war. Maybe a foreigner can only die.

I'm tearing up images of my new home and gluing them back together. The seam makes them poetry. The seam can't be sutured.

I'm cutting up my exotic photographs for the book. I'm using texts about "the flowery kingdom" of China from 1874. It starts out: "It is almost impossible to describe the imperial palace..." But then it goes on to describe it: "with its nine great courts, marble doors and roofs glittering in gold..." I love impossible descriptions. I love how it makes holes in the surface. When I was 25 I put out cigarettes on my own hand.

The Underworld: I wear my shitty Orpheus mask because he was nostalgic. He was torn to pieces when he returned.

Thought about those images of destruction caught by Miman in *Aniara*. In Martinsson's book the destruction of the Earth short-circuits Miman and leaves the people in despair. Might it not have been better this way, might it not have liberated them to finally embrace their aimless flight to know that their home no longer existed. That there was nothing left to go back to. I have to admit, when I stood there in front of my old home, I pictured burning it. I imagined—I daydreamed—the smell of gasoline on my trembling hands. But now I'm stuck in the Solaris dilemma, pretending I'm home. I can never quite get home. I keep walking, keep smelling the fields, keep staring at the buildings, people, listening to the music. I'm home. But I'm not quite there. I can't quite get there. Not without gasoline.

To go home and to go some place utterly different: Why do these sensations feel so similar? I write 13 poems imitating Yi-Sang.

Last night in Malmö. Thought about science fiction and fashion. Imagined deer antlers. Thought about Bruno K Öijer's famous poem about the black puzzle, the wounded animal, the poison. Went back to the tree. Of course it wasn't speaking to me. Thought about burning it down but realized I wouldn't know how to. Thought about how angry it makes people in the US when I talk about being an immigrant. Thought about poison. Thought about why I hate dancing. Saw a child steal candy and get caught. Thought: Are you joking? The messages from Joyelle are like voices from outside a dream. I'm in it. The reverse ghost.

DAY 30

Had a dream about the tree in the People's Park. It was telling me about the new millennium. Then moths fluttered in my face. It was telling me about its sap. I wanted to cut it but I didn't have a knife. Or I had a knife but the blade was too blunt.

The train-ride is one of the greatest forms of modern poetry. It's the reverse film. I'm flickering past a world like Blaise Cendrars. But trains are old now. Film doesn't even exist anymore. I take a selfie by the soccer stadium.

The Göteborg Bookfair is enormous. Like the AWP, but more glamorous. Carl-Michael is full of joy. Invited me and Aase to a shrimp-sandwhich luncheon on the top floor of the conference center. We're giving a reading and q-and-a in Stockholm together.

The Sugar Book disgusts me. It's how I know it's working.

I've never been in Göteborg before. I already feel sad to be moving away from Malmö, Skåne, where I've written so well.

Where I've discovered the true pornographic atmosphere of the book, its true language (counterfeited, contaminated). But it's also true that my grandmother's family is from Göteborg, so perhaps I've finally come home. There's a square named after my great-great grandfather. I should look it up. But the bookfair is downtown and I don't know how much exploring I'll want to do.

In the Göteborg Bookfair, I know so many people who I don't actually know. I follow Aase through the crowd. I don't actually know her. I'm following her. Going home has made me into a follower. A detective of sorts. Or someone who prays. I believe in corruption. Believe it will bring me finally home.

I worry about money, so I buy some kefir. Take it back to the hotel room. Stare at it. So I go buy some wine. Drink it. Like it's summer.

For Norén the actor has to be their own knife: What Norén wants is for the acting to be like the cutting. It's not enough that he cuts away the excesses, he is the knife that does the cutting. The actor cannot act, everything that is "not necessary" has to be "cut" away. But what is "not necessary"? Acting itself. Acting as an inherent excessive. Norén's way around this: to make his art the art of cutting. It's both the disease and the cure.

All these thoughts about Norén: I'm writing a kind of diary but it's also a diary of writing a diary, of reading a diary. A parasite text.

My daughters want a dog. They're making Joyelle sign a contract. When are you coming home, she writes.

Perhaps *The Sugar Book* is just a book of spectacular crime scenes. There is no reason for what happens. There is no psychology, no currency, only transmutation. The narrative fails. I can tell this poem because I'm sick. In this poem I have diabetes, the sugar sickness. I can't remember who you are. I come from someplace else. I'm tearing up exotic photographs.

Not an interiority but a mutation. I read it with my skin. It's dark matter: a pornography of trying to beat myself out of myself. The blue flower, Novalis, pornography-as-event, tourism-as-montage.

My hands seem to want something from me. Want me to decorate them. Want me to bring them in contact with the violence of utopia. I'm here, I tell them. No you're not, they seem to say. I'm ideally suited for this, I think. I will call it Los Angeles.

On July 18, Norén buys Armani underwear.

DAY 31

Just read Gabrielle Wittkop's brilliant novel *The Necrophiliac*.[3]
It does everything US literary establishment tries to forbid: a
sensational, gothic tale about necrophilia written in beautiful-
ly overwrought prose. In his book *Radio Corpse*, Daniel Tif-
fany argues that Ezra Pound wanted to rid modern literature
of the "corpse language" of the Victorians—but ended up as
a fascist. The Conceptualists write that poetry is necrophilic.
Wittkop's book is the most brilliant reply: a truly anti-fascist
poem written in the necrophilic "corpse language" of poetry.

The book claims to be about necrophilia but it's about art.
The corpses are arranged in poses by the solitary artist-narra-
tor, which he then describes in the most ornate prose. On the
very first page she compares a corpse of "a very beautiful dead
girl" to "Chinese porcelain" and notes that "the transparent
lips" are "a pale mauve." She calls the corpses' breaths "bom-
byx": it's the name of the silk moth but it sounds like onyx,
like something elaborately artificial. The corpses exhale art.

The silk moth: the ultimate icon of Art and also of its ob-
scene father, Imperialism.

I was thrilled to find that the last victims, the ultimate
love objects of this necrophiliac, were two Swedish twins,

---

[3] Translated by Don Bapst.

found drowned. The necrophiliac imagines that they were incestuous and therefore chose to kill themselves. Here two fantasies of Swedes come together: the idea of whiteness as natural and the idea of whiteness as artifice. The twin Swedes manage to be not just both female and male but also innocent and taboo-transgressing, natural and artificial.

From *The Necrophiliac*: "I become another person. I'm suddenly a stranger to myself." The protagonist of the book says this when he's pulling off his deed. It's noteworthy that Norén keep saying almost exactly the same words when he's writing. He constantly has to become a stranger to himself. And then here I am: back home, trying to write my impossible book about being a foreigner. Maybe it's an impossible book about looking in the mirror.

Was supposed to go dancing but walked around the soccer stadium instead. It was smaller than I remembered but somehow when I started walking I had to keep on walking. It was like I had entered an in-between space. I could see the part of town with all the restaurants, glowing in the near distance but something kept me from even going there. I was stuck in an alternative reality. It was frightening and saddening but I didn't want to leave, didn't want to be part of the world. I thought: This is what a ghost must feel like. But then I thought: It's the other way around. They're the ghosts. Keep telling yourself that, you ghost.

My wife writes me a note. The kids are watching "it's nightmare night in ponyville." She's listening to Big Star. Calls it "beautiful suicide music."

DAY 32

What's the purpose of going on and on, of going on too long. It's one of the things *Publishers Weekly* objected to about *Haute Surveillance*: it went on for too long. It's what made the book not only pornographic but failed pornography, a "morass." Like the porno after orgasm, it has to do with the beauty of the dragged-out, the aftermath. Carl Michael calls it the "parapornographic": art's slag, art's drag.

Establishments must always maintain their gold standards. Must always guard against inflation. Which is why translation makes its critics so nervous: too many versions, by too many authors, from too many traditions. It's the "plague ground" Joyelle wrote about.

The Sugar Book takes place in the aftermath: after the crash, after the plague, after the riots. Takes place in ruin porn. I think about the LA arts collective Asco's photograph "First Supper (After a Major Riot)" where the members sit on the median of Whittier Blvd in makeup and masks. I'm sampling the crime reports from the LA riots. I'm dys-translating them. *Die sunflower die.*

Norén's diary is seeping into *The Sugar Book*. I write about Solaris when I feel homesick. Sara has entered my book as a kind of debased, baroque version of Francesca Woodman. An icon of art's excess. Every other poem is about Norén's shopping sprees. *The Sugar Book* is a parasite's diary. Art is the parasite. Lars Norén is the host.

Aase called. Wanted to meet before I went to Stockholm. I wanted to leave before her so I said we'd meet in Stockholm. At the train station leaving Göteborg I called Magdalena again. Still no answer. I left another foolish message. Funny, all this time I saw myself as Orpheus, but I'm the angel.

Thought about those summers at the beach.

DAY 33

Stockholm is so beautiful at 5 am.

Norén loves Anselm Kiefer. I can see why: Paintings as ruins. Always the angels nearby, threatening to turn it all into kitsch.

Wrote fantastic today. To celebrate I walked down to the water and spent evening reading Defoe's plague book. Started copying down passages. Started rewriting them to be about a different kind of plague. I love the stupid science: breathe on a mirror. If there are worms on the mirror, you have the plague. Sounds like the stupid—but precise!—science of druggies. I love drug culture but I can't stand the sickness. If I wasn't such a weakling, I would be a druggie. Why not crash this whole world through a mirror. Take me to Cocteauland.

If the artist becomes a stranger—and possibly dead—in the act of art-making, the artwork itself partakes in a similar dynamic. Wittkop writes about the Swedish twins: "They resembled each other in an indescribable way and had no doubt been twins." Rather than estrangement, death brings them into resemblance. In the act of art, the artist becomes another, contaminated by the "bombyx" of the dead, but the other doubles, resembles, becomes *like*.[4] The very next sentence complicates the image: "Death had changed the quality of their tans, which the salt had frosted into a gold of a strange, subtle pallor comparable to that given off by a candle flame." They are transformed into likeness by death: something strange, something like a fashion shoot, that doubles, analogizes. Like Laura Palmer with pearls on her forehead, wrapped in plastic. Dead Swedish twins are the most poetical topic in the world.

Altering Blanchot's analogy comparing image to corpse, in Wittkop's book the corpse becomes Art: "Their sexes: two infant mollusks." If *The Necrophiliac* is pornographic, it is not pornographic only in its formal deviance (as in Sontag's special category of "high" pornographic literature)—with its extravagant syntax, its molluscular imagery stalling any kind of personal "growth" or redemption in the narrator—or in the conventionally pornographic definition (although the entire story focuses on describing sexual acts), but also in a parapornographic way: artifice and the body—the two realms which are opposed in traditional pornography (we want the clothes to be removed from the naked body)—become unified in the bombyx atmosphere. The naked body becomes both the object of sexual feelings and a work of art.

This transformative, deadly power of strangeness is constantly played out on the pages of Norén's diary. On almost every page, Norén repeats the urge on one hand to become *strange* and on the other hand for his art, his apartment, his cottage in Gotland to be *simple*. It's surprising because I associate

---

[4] In Swedish, the word for corpse is "lik."

Norén's work with the excessive, over-the-top, even baroque. Six hour plays. Poems that incorporate entire Beatles songs. "Schizopoetics": poems piled up in plastic bags. Perhaps it was an urge toward purity that drove him all along. Perhaps it's what drives me as I write this sugar book. No, it's the opposite. I want to turn purity into matter. I'm not clean. That's the greatest betrayal. I'm writing a treasonous text.

DAY 34

I have a new bump on my head. I'm bound to be a monster, my whole head and face will be a bubbling mess. I still remember that day in Minneapolis, in high school, when Tyler and I drove past the salvation army store downtown and I saw a guy whose face seemed to melt and in that instance I became convinced that my face too would melt like that, that by looking I had become infected by his disease. It's happening. It's just a question if I will actually die before I become that monstrous.

Norén discusses a made-for-TV movie that accuses *7:3* of having directly caused the murders in Malexander. A little later, Norén reads op-ed pieces that argue that Norén was the "fourth killer." It's an absurd argument but art is always potentially "the fourth killer." That's part of its power.

As Bataille said, poetry is the most profound luxury. When the journalists want Norén to "take responsibility" of the crime, what they're saying is that they want him to reject art's art-ness. They want him to return to a restricted economy that can never truly contain poetry.

These op-eds lead Norén someplace unexpected: "Should I write poetry again? I really just wanted to write a daily journal about the work of being a dramatist and director. Facts, times, concrete information about meetings and about who and about what. No thoughts, images, dreams, no love, no Tidaholm. Only concrete facts, nothing else. I am trying to counteract all those other things in order to come back to it again, but it's impossible. Since I am invaded with it. Where resistance ends, hell begins..." One way of reading the diary then is as an act of eradicating poetry—or "dreams"— through facts, through the protestant work ethics, but this way fails, resulting in the "hell" of poetry. Poetry is what has to be eradicated for a clean world.

Found this quote from Jean Genet's *Thief's Journal*: "Then I really felt I was in exile, and my nervousness was going to make me permeable to what—for want of other words—I shall call poetry."[5]

Poetry against all.

Once I wrote a poem for Magdalena. I was in my mid twenties. It's like I didn't think about her, the beach, the bumble bees for many years and then it seeped back in my head. In the poem, I walk under water, on all fours, across the Atlantic. Of course it's not the Atlantic. It's the River Styx. Magdalena knows this, and it's why she won't answer her phone. She refuses to interact with the dead. She refuses to be dead.

---

[5] Translated by Bernard Frechtman.

Walking over to meet a film director (who's made a movie about Johan Jönson) for coffee it struck me that I am neither native nor tourist, that my struggles come from the fact that I'm stuck in between these two more stable poles. Nervous like when I looked at the Woodman photographs. Nervous like poetry.

The exotic is a stabilizing gaze for a foreignness that is far too volatile. It's a way of domesticating the foreign—as foreign. This quarantine always fails. I have known this since I was 13 years old.

Is it the case that as I walk around Stockholm what I want is to be infected? Or else I'll have to imagine the city's utter destruction.

Passed foreign beggar who shouted in English after me: "Go home you Coca-Cola-sucking fucker!" I wanted to turn around and explain that I *was* home but I didn't. I wasn't. I hate Coca-Cola. I can't go home. Ruins.

Ghosts must walk a lot. Must be why we are called "gengångare." The repeat walkers. Walked all the way across the South of Stockholm today. But stopped before I reached Johannes Hov, where my grandmother used to live. But that's not why I stopped. I stopped because I felt stupid.

DAY 35

The speaking tree appeared to me in another dream. This time I was quicker. I took down every word on my arm. When I woke up, it had been smudged. But I remember what it said. This will not go in the book.

The Sugar Book disturbs me. Now that pop song is playing again. The one with ballgowns dripping blood. The corpse of poetry: When Conceptual poets claim to have "killed poetry" I don't think of it as one dead body, but hundreds scattering the landscape. That's probably why Josef Kaplan's *Kill List* had to go on and on. They have to constantly reiterate that they've killed it. I didn't kill it. I'm writing a kind of dead poetry.

I'm doing the twist, the stuffed fox, the emigrant. The disease I carry within me isn't within me. Beat me out of me.

What happened to all the stuff I wrote in Korea all night long when I couldn't sleep? If I didn't burn it (and I most certainly did not), I should have. I wish I had that material now. Seoul as a kind of afterworld for *The Sugar Book*. Or rather pre-world. I became unmoored. I wish I had the record of that unmooring. It would be comforting because it would allow me to located it in time and place. I'm still in Korea.

Saw a Nathalie Djurberg video at the Modern Museum. Like Sara's work, it seems pornographically, grotesquely without interiority. The agency is as much in the clay that makes up the figures as in some idea of interiority. I think about that character from Don DeLillo's *Great Jones Street*: pornography for children.

Got an unexpected call from Mathias. He said Magdalena was busy. She has just met her true love, got a divorce from the father of her children and is sorting everything out. Mathias was telling me about his own life. He too was divorced, currently living in Northern Sweden, filming what I understood to be part documentary and part reality TV show about elder care. We reminisced for a while but then I had to leave to go meet Aase. It was nice but strangely anticlimactic to speak to him. I can't help thinking that because I left the country, I put much more pressure on my childhood than they do. They moved on, had full lives. I have spent my entire life obsessed with my childhood. I wondered if Mathias called to spare Magdalena dealing with a crazy person from when she was a child. I remembered when she taught me about the jellyfish. How she held it in the palm of her hand.

I noticed a long straw of hair sticking to my cardigan. I pulled it off the cardigan and inspected in closer. It was black. It was certainly Joyelle's hair. I started looking at all my clothes, pulling black hair from each one until I had a pile of black hair in front of me. I wet it down with my own saliva and knitted out of them a new sweater. A sweater to keep one safe while singing in the underworld.

DAY 36

I wish I could watch a documentary tonight. Or Jan Troell's film about The Åmsele Murders. I must have watched a bit of it because I have an impression of it. Kind of like Gus Van Zandt's movie about the Columbine Murders—surprisingly formalist, quiet, beautiful. Perhaps it's the similar situation: art about a public trauma.

The Åmsele Murders: I remember them. I was back home that summer. I was in Torekov with Måns, falling in love with those sisters who were staying with their grandmother in Båstad, listening to Imperiet's *Synd*. I drank a bottle of dandelion wine and we all went skinny-dipping in the ocean while nearby two Finnish youngsters tried to escape the cops chasing them through the countryside.

Troell's movie was called *Il Capitano*. I've found some of it on youtube. It begins with a strange image of a cat-like face and sand or powder heaping up. Then an interrogation of the woman. At first face to face. Then: as voice-over while the film shows the beautiful northern landscape. They talk about fear. The interrogator asks her: How did you meet? There's an abrupt change. She's waiting for the bus. He hectors her into getting in his car. They speak in Finnish, no subtitles.

I can't understand what they say. They travel to a wreckage yard where the trains pass by. Everything is wet and muddy. In his room, he romances her by playing a shitty acoustic guitar and showing her his sketchbooks of neo-Nazi, skateboard fantasias. The criminal is always an artist, the artist a criminal. Cut back to the interrogator, who says: Not very impressive crime record. Stolen car. Stolen car. Drunk driving. The expressionist art from his room counteracted by the poetry-is-dead conceptual poetry of his crime record. The real mug shot. The interrogator: He seems like a talentless little thief. Minna: He told me he was going to do something big. There is always the view of the law which reduces everybody, and makes every artist "talentless" unless he or she has been made famous, acceptable by the establishment, and the private, always grandiose fantasies of the young person with unreasonable dreams. In the view of the law, he is talentless, someone who steals (even his outfit looks like it's been taken from Gary Oldman's portrayal of Sid Vicious), but in his own mind there's a violence against the law: the great act. Cut. Another flashback—this time it has nothing to do with her, a flashback in Jari's mind, although he's not present in the "frame narrative" of the interrogation—of grade school when the class photos are handed out. He isn't visible, hidden behind another student. He talks to the teacher, gets angry, smashes up the photo and leaves the classroom. He runs across the train tracks into a *Stalker*-like hangar with scattered junk and gets into a junky car. Takes out a pen and the class photo and circles his occluded face as if to say: I exist. This could be read as giving interiority, psychologizing the crimes—and that's probably the best reading—but I also want to see it as a very direct, material movement: He is erased and he uses the pen—art—to assert his own existence. The next scene he is driving a stolen truck around the schoolyard then taking off chased by police. This, the film argues, is how it begins. Cut to black-and-white footage of young people rioting against police. Apparently they travelled to Copenhagen. The interrogator asks her about an abortion. She says: Jari liked it there. There was no hope. We didn't have to hope.

I love that line. We didn't have to hope.

DAY 37

According to the Internet Troell was present at the trial of the murderers. When asked what he was doing there, he said he was going to make a film about the case. People were enraged and protested even though he had not even begun to shoot the film. Three years later, he did release the film to mixed critical reaction. Jan Aghed at Sydsvenskan called him a "poet" of cinema, but *Aftonbladet*'s Jan Olov Andersson said the movie "felt superficial." Did they mean the same thing? Andersson also objected to the fact that Troell did not show the faces of the victims as they were being killed. It was both pornography and bad pornography at the same time. A movie made without hope.

The idea that to make art about a violent event is immoral because it somehow cheapens the event is widespread. It's the thesis of Friedlander's book (art becomes kitsch). After the school massacre at Sandy Hook, Blake and I wrote a play called "Sandy" about violence in America and nobody wanted to publish it. Even presses and journals that had been begging us for work before now found our text "offensive." It is as if art cannot comment on the contemporary without becoming pornographic. Art is treated merely as a representation that cheapens.

Reading Aase's essay "Tsunami from Solaris," where she talks about Swedish Radio censoring her poem because its surreal language might cause listeners to think about the recent tsunami in Thailand. Meanwhile, TV showed images of the disaster over and over. It was the poem with its tangled images that were deemed pornographic, not the TV reports, since they were deemed documentary. The problem was not that the poem was about Thailand, it was that it was deemed a "bad copy." An evil copy that would both cheapen the event and make it too potent.

The tsunami wave is of course also a derailed copy: a UFO-wave that burst into the normal human ocean. It is a wave that doesn't understand how to be a normal wave and attacks all the tourist beaches and the not-everyday-people's plagiarized, artificial paradise (the everyday inhabitants in the hit countries worked and were not living in paradise, so maybe death was closer to their reality). It is as if the tsunami wave was set in motion by the ocean on the planet Solaris in Stanislaw Lem's novel."

—Aase Berg

Solaris is poetry itself. The tsunami is poetry itself. How can on carry on with cruel poetry when the sense of security is collapsing and what reminds one of reality is more horrifying than the real? Why is similarity scarier than authenticity? Why is the copy more dangerous than the original? Why is the poem such an insult to this evil life?"

—Aase Berg

There is a peculiar symbiosis between the artificial public sorrow which has to eliminate artifice, the deathless paradise of Swedish welfare state, and the paradise of the beaches of Thailand. Art has a kind of antisocial force that perverts "paradises." I might say that the bad copy is an antidote to paradise. The bad copy perverts. It is a poem written without hope. Poetry against all.

DAY 38

The reading went well. We read and talked. Johan Jönson asked if we weren't after all "immanentist." I don't know what that means, but I said, yes, I'm probably an immanentist because I believe in poetry against all.

Afterwards Madeleine Grieve took me and Aase out for drinks. We talked about the gurlesque, Ann Jäderlund, Kim Hyesoon, the latest US poetry, Nathalie Djurberg, Kara Walker. We decided that the next issue of *10tal* would focus on the gurlesque. That the next Stockholm Poetry Festival would also focus on the gurlesque. Incredible feeling to suddenly be offered the pages of a journal I grew up reading.

Today I went over and met with Madeleine again. We concocted this incredible plan for the gurlesque issue of *10tal*: an international gathering point for contemporary writers like Kim Hyesoon, Kim Yideum, Olga Ravn and Chelsey Minnis. I told her I would write an essay on the gurlesque use of kitsch and violence.

What Aase calls the poetry of the "bad copy," Solaris-poetry, are different words for kitsch. Kitsch is the bad copy, the version, the inauthentic. Versions have the capacity to become derailed, to become a storm, or, as Joyelle wrote, a "plague ground." The plague ground: this is what the literary establishment fears most of all. Contamination and proliferation. Poetry against all.

Norén talks so much about ruins and people becoming ruins. Then he becomes a ruin himself. Gets some kind of tooth infection and the German dentist cuts part of his jaw away. Goes to the Swedish dentist who think the German doctor messed up. Cut too much bone off the jaw. Now he has to have all his teeth pulled to stop the "degeneration." But also his play seems to be in ruins—"collapsing like sand" at the end. Perhaps he should let it collapse. Let it become pornography. Or poetry.

DAY 39

In humanistic thinking, Art is proof of the human soul. Counterfeits cannot write poetry. But there's another art: the art of the robot, the alien, the mimic. The bad copy. These artworks move in waves.

Another way of putting this is in Leo Bersani's terms: the bad copy is against "the culture of redemption," the dominant, reparative model of art as something that can redeem history. Redeem art. Unredeemed art is pornographic. It has no hope.

I think of Ranciere's quote: "the production of a sensory form of strangeness."

I think about the beach—about Mathias and Magdalena—but then I stop myself because it's just Solaris visions.

I have to write this book to cut them away.

I can't cut them away, it would be a betrayal of my aesthetics.

I will restage *The Necrophiliac* in Los Angeles as a tourist book.

They will be the Swedish twins.

A bad copy. A strange copy. Poetry against all.

Why am I sitting in my shitty hotel room in Stockholm writing fantasies about the underworld? Or do I mean "undergången"? The Swedish—"the going-under"—sounds so much more evocative than "the apocalypse." I mean a world without hope.

DAY 40

Norén is thinking about staging plays by Sarah Kane. He seems to feel ambivalent. His ex C says Kane is too "pubertal" and Norén writes, "Yes, she is." But he "likes the language, the brutality, the total directness and most of all the necessity of everything she writes." I hate when US poets start talking about directness because they inevitably mean some kind of interiority, making the poet's soul legible to the reader. But Norén is talking about the violence of directness. How it hits the spectator. That is all I care about when I write. Poetry against all.

On June 17th, Norén writes: "Why am I writing this book? Am I writing it instead of committing suicide?"

I'm only halfway through Norén's diary but I'm almost done with *The Sugar Book*. I have 400 pages of poetry. I could write it endlessly. Just give me some words and I'll turn it into sugar. But I don't want it to be monumental like Norén. I don't want that kind of authority. I want the cover to look like Joyelle's fancy Japanese soap, Tokyo Milk: black with a white silhouette of a moth, bombyx.

The only way this pornographic sugar book can develop is through proliferation. I'm rewriting *The Journal of a Plague Year* into my own book. This fictional plague, like the fictional tsunami will ruin my book again.

DAY 41

Several of Norén's plays are available on the Swedish TV homepage. I don't have the patience for them—whether they are set in a hotel or in Hades. But there's an interesting, black-and-white interview from the 1970s, a young Norén is interviewed while walking around in rural ruins. Exactly the kind I imagine *Revolver* taking place in. He plays a wrecked piano inside one falling-apart ball room. They're asking him about his novel, *The Bee Keepers*. He's telling them he writes in ruins.

I am rewriting *The Sugar Book* with Norén as my reader—a reader who hates me, who wants to cut my poems. I'm not succumbing to his aesthetic or rejecting it—I'm letting it attract me, draw me toward it—but I'm also resisting it. I'm writing a book that stages a struggle for its own elimination.

DAY 42

In one of the most beautiful passages of his diaries, Norén writes: "Soon I will begin to write harder, more nakedly, shorter. Beyond the mist. Scenes as from overexposed photographs. Dialogues that could have been caught on a surveillance camera. Movement, physics, behaviorism. I long for the light that is called merciless. I am heading there. When everything is over."

He needs to make art that annihilates itself. He can only save art from itself by cutting it. I'm doing the opposite. No. I have to do the same. I have to hate myself in this book. Mirror book. Fainting book. All these pages have to be cut. Cutting will be its own excess.

Norén asks: "How can I become a stranger again? And a stranger to myself? I became that when I began to write drama because I didn't know how to do that." I want to tell him he becomes a stranger when his face falls apart. When he looks in the mirror. When he writes his plays. It's why he wants to cut them. I understand how he feels. The more I go into this sugar book the stranger I become. I'm cutting the book, not just poems, but lines, words. I'm making the whole thing slimmer. I'm being merciless.

December 12, 2001. The German press hates Norén's Berlin play, says its "more kitsch than morality," that it "falls apart." Like his face, I would add. Like pornography always does, I would add. History destroys every diorama.

DAY 43

I have a picture of myself in my head. It won't go away. In the picture I'm wearing headphones. I think about stabbing it. It won't go away.

Had lunch with my uncle who gave me a bunch of old photographs of grandmother, told me to pick one. I took one of her in her 20s, very young and glamorous. On the back it was stamped Berlin, 1936. I asked my uncle what she was doing in Berlin at that date. He told me she was a Nazi sympathizer, that she had met my grandfather at a Nazi youth rally in her early 20s, gotten pregnant and been forced to marry him. My uncle always drinks rosé. As if it's always summer. We sat there on his deck in a suburb full of refugees from the Middle East and the Balkan Peninsula, drinking rosé in the sunlight. It is always summer when I see him.

December 26, 2001: "They don't have any snow in Paris, they have oysters." (Norén)

DAY 44

I remember in Korea how beautiful the light was.

I remember in Korea the octopus in the aquarium.

I remember in Korea the meat protest.

I remember in Korea how beautiful the light was.

I think I'm finished with *The Sugar Book*. I let the boy out of his prison. I let him into the infection of Los Angeles. It was the only way I could finish the book. I let him out because I was cutting everything. I was turning it into a cutter's book.

Tomorrow I'm going back to the US.

It's a relief to walk through Stockholm and know that every-thing is finished.

In my neighborhood there's an official sign that reads "This Area Is Under Surveillance" and somebody had slapped a sticker that said "MY HEART IS A BOMB!"

This is written without hope.
Poetry against all.

October, 2013

ACKNOWLEDGEMENTS

These diary entries were first written to be part of *The Sugar Book*, but I cut them from the manuscript because they seemed too personal. I first published an excerpt of the manuscript when Michael Slozek asked me for writing for the Poetry Foundation website. Great thanks to Michael for publishing the excerpt, and to Christian Peet, who had the idea that it might be a whole book.

I also want to thank Thomas Grandi, Sara Tuss Efrik, Sten Barnekow, Aase Berg, Kristian Carlsson, Leif Holmstrand, Clemens Altgård and Martin Glaz Serup for their support and friendship during the writing of this book.

And greatest thanks to Joyelle McSweeney for her constant inspiration.

ABOUT THE AUTHOR

Johannes Göransson is the author of six books of poetry and the critical book *Transgressive Circulation: Essays On Translation*. Among the poets he has translated are Aase Berg, Helena Boberg, Kim Yideum and Ann Jäderlund. Together with Joyelle McSweeney, he edits Action Books. He teaches at the University of Notre Dame in South Bend, Indiana.

TARPAULIN SKY PRESS

Warped from one world to another. (*THE NATION*) Somewhere between Artaud and Lars Von Trier. (*VICE*) Hallucinatory...trance-inducing.... A kind of nut job's notebook....Harnesses the throbbing pulse of language itself....Playful, experimental appeal....Unrelenting, grotesque beauty. (*PUBLISHERS WEEKLY*) Simultaneously metaphysical and visceral....Scary, sexual, and intellectually disarming. (*HUFFINGTON POST*) Horrifying and humbling.... (*THE RUMPUS*) Wholly new. (*IOWA REVIEW*) ....only becomes more surreal. (*NPR BOOKS*) The opposite of boring.... An ominous conflagration devouring the bland terrain of conventional realism.... Dangerous language, a murderous kind ... discomfiting, filthy, hilarious, and ecstatic. (*BOOKSLUT*) Creating a zone where elegance and grace can gambol with the just-plain-fucked-up. (*HTML GIANT*) Uncomfortably enjoyable. (*AMERICAN BOOK REVIEW*) Consistently inventive. (*TRIQUARTERLY*) A peculiar, personal music that is at once apart from and very much surrounded by the world. (*VERSE*) A world of wounded voices. (*HYPERALLERGIC*) Futile, sad, and beautiful. (*NEWPAGES*) Inspired and unexpected. Highly recommended. (*AFTER ELLEN*)

MORE FROM TS PRESS >>

REBECCA BROWN
NOT HEAVEN, SOMEWHERE ELSE

If heaven is somewhere, it isn't with us, but somewhere we want to get — a state, a place, a turning to home. Novel- and essayist Rebecca Brown's thirteenth book is narrative cycle that revamps old fairy tales, movies, and myths, as it leads the reader from darkness to light, from harshness to love, from where we are to where we might go.

PRAISE FOR *NOT HEAVEN, SOMEWHERE ELSE*: "Aside from 'genius,' the other word I would use to describe Rebecca Brown is 'elemental'.... She's a genius at the invisible forces that bind words together.... It feels dangerous and exciting, like if she puts her big brain to it long enough, she could completely rewrite the story of who we are." (PAUL CONSTANT, *SEATTLE REVIEW OF BOOKS*) "Satisfied a desire for moral discussion I didn't even know I had.... Highly recommended and highly rewarding." (RICH SMITH, *THE STRANGER*) PRAISE FOR REBECCA BROWN: "Strips her language of convention to lay bare the ferocious rituals of love and need." (*THE NEW YORK TIMES*) "One of the few truly original modern lesbian writers, one who constantly pushes both her own boundaries and those of her readers." (*SAN FRANCISCO CHRONICLE*) "Watch for her books and hunt down her short stories." (DOROTHY ALLISON) "America's only real rock 'n' roll schoolteacher." (THURSTON MOORE, SONIC YOUTH)

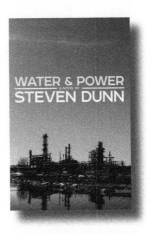

STEVEN DUNN
WATER & POWER

SPD Fiction Bestseller
Featured at *Buzzfeed News*:
"Books That Prove Indie Presses Deserve Your Attention"

Navy veteran Steven Dunn's second novel, *water & power*, plunges into military culture and engages with perceptions of heroism and terrorism. In this shifting landscape, deployments are feared, absurd bureaucracy is normalized, and service members are consecrated. *water & power* is a collage of voices, documents, and critical explorations that disrupt the usual frequency channels of military narratives. "Traversing both horror and humor, Dunn imbues his prose with the kind of duality that is hard to achieve, but pays off." (WENDY J. FOX, *BUZZFEED NEWS*) "Dunn's remarkable talent for storytelling collapses the boundaries between poetry and prose, memoir and fiction." (NIKKI WALLSCHLAEGER) "Captures the difficult, funny, abject, exhilarating, heartbreaking and maddening aspects of Navy life, both on and off duty. Read this book and understand the veterans in your life better, understand the aggressive disconnection the armed forces demands, and retain a much clearer picture of the people who wear the uniform in America's name." (KHADIJAH QUEEN)

JENNIFER S. CHENG
MOON: LETTERS, MAPS, POEMS

Co-winner, Tarpaulin Sky Book Award, chosen by Bhanu Kapil
Publishers Weekly, Starred Review
SPD Poetry Bestseller
Nominated for the PEN American Open Book Award

Mixing fable and fact, extraordinary and ordinary, Jennifer S. Cheng's hybrid collection, *Moon: Letters, Maps, Poems*, draws on various Chinese mythologies about women, particularly that of Chang'E (the Lady in the Moon), uncovering the shadow stories of our myths. "Exhilarating ... An alt-epic for the 21st century ... Visionary ... Rich and glorious." (**PUBLISHERS WEEKLY STARRED REVIEW**) "If reading is a form of pilgrimage, then Cheng gives us its charnel ground events, animal conversions, guiding figures and elemental life." (**BHANU KAPIL**) "Each of the voices in Jennifer S. Cheng's *Moon* speaks as if she's 'the last girl on earth.' ... With curiosity and attention, *Moon* shines its light on inquiry as art, asking as making. In the tradition of Fanny Howe's poetics of bewilderment, Cheng gives us a poetics of possibility." (**JENNIFER TSENG**) "Cheng's newest poetry collection bravely tests language and the beautiful boundaries of body and geography ... A rich and deeply satisfying read." (**AIMEE NEZHUKUMATATHIL**)

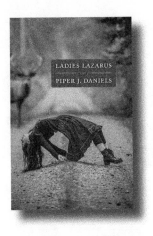

PIPER J. DANIELS
LADIES LAZARUS

Co-winner, Tarpaulin Sky Book Award
Nominated for the PEN/Diamonstein-Spielvogel Award
for the Art of the Essay

Equal parts séance, polemic, and love letter, Piper J. Daniels's *Ladies Lazarus* examines evangelical upbringing, sexual trauma, queer identity, and mental illness with a raw intensity that moves between venom and grace. Fueled by wanderlust, Daniels travels the country, unearthing the voices of forgotten women. Girls and ghosts speak freely, murdered women serve as mentors, and those who've languished in unmarked graves convert their names to psalms. At every turn, Daniels invites the reader to engage, not in the soothing narrative of healing, but in the literal and metaphorical dynamism of death and resurrection. "Beautifully written collection of 11 lyric essays ... Daniels emerges as an empowering and noteworthy voice." (**PUBLISHERS WEEKLY**) "*Ladies Lazarus* is the best debut I've read in a long time. Daniels has resurrected the personal essay and what it is and what it can do." (**JENNY BOULLY**) "An extremely intelligent, impressively understated, and achingly powerful work." (**DAVID SHIELDS**) "A siren song from planet woman, a love letter from the body, a resistance narrative against the dark." (**LIDIA YUKNAVITCH**)

STEVEN DUNN
POTTED MEAT

Co-winner, Tarpaulin Sky Book Award
Shortlist, *Granta*'s "Best of Young American Novelists"
Finalist, Colorado Book Award
SPD Fiction Bestseller

Set in a decaying town in West Virginia, Steven Dunn's debut
novel, *Potted Meat,* follows a boy into adolescence as he struggles
with abuse, poverty, alcoholism, and racial tensions. A meditation
on trauma and the ways in which a person might surivive, if not
thrive, *Potted Meat* examines the fear, power, and vulnerability of
storytelling itself. "101 pages of miniature texts that keep tapping
the nails in, over and over, while speaking as clearly and directly
as you could ask.... Bone Thugs, underage drinking, alienation,
death, love, Bob Ross, dreams of blood.... Flooded with power."
(**BLAKE BUTLER,** *VICE MAGAZINE*) "Full of wonder and silence
and beauty and strangeness and ugliness and sadness....This book
needs to be read." (**LAIRD HUNT**) "A visceral intervention across
the surface of language, simultaneously cutting to its depths, to
change the world.... I feel grateful to be alive during the time in
which Steven Dunn writes books." (**SELAH SATERSTROM**)

ELIZABETH HALL
I HAVE DEVOTED MY LIFE TO THE CLITORIS

Co-winner, Tarpaulin Sky Book Award
Finalist, Lambda Literary Award for Bisexual Nonfiction
SPD Nonfiction Bestseller

Debut author Elizabeth Hall set out to read everything that has been written about the clitoris. The result is "Freud, terra cotta cunts, hyenas, anatomists, and Acker, mixed with a certain slant of light on a windowsill and a leg thrown open invite us. Bawdy and beautiful." (**WENDY C. ORTIZ**). "An orgy of information ... rendered with graceful care, delivering in small bites an investigation of the clit that is simultaneously a meditation on the myriad ways in which smallness hides power." (*THE RUMPUS*) "Marvelously researched and sculpted.... bulleted points rat-tat-tatting the patriarchy, strobing with pleasure." (**DODIE BELLAMY**) "Philosophers and theorists have always asked what the body is—Hall just goes further than the classical ideal of the male body, beyond the woman as a vessel or victim, past genre as gender, to the clitoris. And we should follow her." (*KENYON REVIEW*) "Gorgeous little book about a gorgeous little organ.... The 'tender button' finally gets its due." (**JANET SARBANES**) "You will learn and laugh .... God this book is glorious." (**SUZANNE SCANLON**)

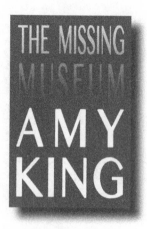

AMY KING
THE MISSING MUSEUM

Co-winner, Tarpaulin Sky Book Award
SPD Poetry Bestseller

Nothing that is complicated may ever be simplified, but rather catalogued, cherished, exposed. *The Missing Museum* spans art, physics & the spiritual, including poems that converse with the sublime and ethereal. They act through ekphrasis, apostrophe & alchemical conjuring. They amass, pile, and occasionally flatten as matter is beaten into text. Here is a kind of directory of the world as it rushes into extinction, in order to preserve and transform it at once. "Understanding' is not a part of the book's project, but rather a condition that one must move through like a person hurriedly moving through a museum." (*PUBLISHERS WEEKLY*) "Women's National Book Association Award-winner Amy King balances passages that can prompt head-scratching wonder with a direct fusillade of shouty caps.... You're not just seeing through her eyes but, perhaps more importantly, breathing through her lungs." (*LAMBDA LITERARY*) "A visceral stunner ... and an instruction manual.... King's archival work testifies to the power—however obscured by the daily noise of our historical moment—of art, of the possibility for artists to legislate the world." (*KENYON REVIEW*)

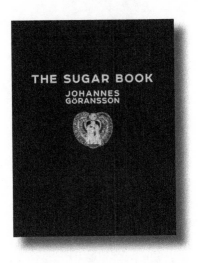

JOHANNES GÖRANSSON
THE SUGAR BOOK

SPD Poetry Bestseller

Johannes Göransson's *The Sugar Book* marks the author's third title with TS Press, following his acclaimed *Haute Surveillance* and *entrance to a colonial pageant in which we all begin to intricate.* "Doubling down on his trademark misanthropic imagery amid a pageantry of the unpleasant, Johannes Göransson strolls through a violent Los Angeles in this hybrid of prose and verse…. The motifs are plentiful and varied … pubic hair, Orpheus, law, pigs, disease, Francesca Woodman … and the speaker's hunger for cocaine and copulation….. Fans of Göransson's distorted poetics will find this a productive addition to his body of work". (**PUBLISHERS WEEKLY**) "Sends its message like a mail train. Visceral Surrealism. His end game is an exit wound." (**FANZINE**) "As savagely anti-idealist as Burroughs or Guyotat or Ballard. Like those writers, he has no interest in assuring the reader that she or he lives, along with the poet, on the right side of history." (**ENTROPY MAGAZINE**) "Convulses wildly like an animal that has eaten the poem's interior and exterior all together with silver." (**KIM HYESOON**) "'I make a language out of the bleed-through.' Göransson sure as fuck does. These poems made me cry. So sad and anxious and genius and glarey bright." (**REBECCA LOUDON**)

AARON APPS
INTERSEX

"Favorite Nonfiction of 2015," Dennis Cooper
SPD Bestseller and Staff Pick

Intersexed author Aaron Apps's hybrid-genre memoir adopts and upends historical descriptors of hermaphroditic bodies such as "imposter," "sexual pervert," "freak of nature," and "unfortunate monstrosity," tracing the author's own monstrous sex as it perversely intertwines with gender expectations and medical discourse. "Graphic vignettes involving live alligators, diarrhea in department store bathrooms, domesticity, dissected animals, and the medicalization of sex.... Unafraid of failure and therefore willing to employ risk as a model for confronting violence, living with it, learning from it." (*AMERICAN BOOK REVIEW*) "I felt this book in the middle of my own body. Like the best kind of memoir, Apps brings a reader close to an experience of life that is both 'unattainable' and attentive to 'what will emerge from things.' In doing so, he has written a book that bursts from its very frame." (BHANU KAPIL)

Excerpts from *Intersex* were nominated for a Pushcart Prize by *Carolina Quarterly*, and appear in *Best American Essays 2014*.

CLAIRE DONATO
BURIAL

A debut novella that slays even seasoned readers. Set in the mind of a narrator who is grieving the loss of her father, who conflates her hotel room with the morgue, and who encounters characters that may not exist, *Burial* is a little story about an immeasurable black hole; an elegy in prose at once lyrical and intelligent, with no small amount of rot and vomit and ghosts. "Poetic, trance-inducing language turns a reckoning with the confusion of mortality into readerly joy at the sensuality of living." (*Publishers Weekly* "Best Summer Reads") "A dark, multivalent, genre-bending book.... Unrelenting, grotesque beauty an exhaustive recursive obsession about the unburiability of the dead, and the incomprehensibility of death." (*Publishers Weekly* Starred Review) "Dense, potent language captures that sense of the unreal that, for a time, pulls people in mourning to feel closer to the dead than the living.... Sartlingly original and effective." (*Minneapolis Star-Tribune*) "A grief-dream, an attempt to un-sew pain from experience and to reveal it in language." (*HTML Giant*) "A full and vibrant illustration of the restless turns of a mind undergoing trauma.... Donato makes and unmakes the world with words, and what is left shimmers with pain and delight." (Brian Evenson) "A gorgeous fugue, an unforgettable progression, a telling I cannot shake." (Heather Christle) "Claire Donato's assured and poetic debut augurs a promising career." (Benjamin Moser)

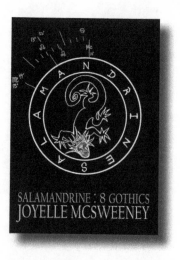

JOYELLE MCSWEENEY
SALAMANDRINE: 8 GOTHICS

Following poet and playwright Joyelle McSweeney's acclaimed novels *Flet*, from Fence Books, and *Nylund, The Sarcographer*, from Tarpaulin Sky Press, comes a collection of shorter prose texts by McSweeney, *Salamandrine: 8 Gothics*, perhaps better described as a series of formal/generic lenses refracting the dread and isolation of contemporary life and producing a distorted, attenuated, spasmatic experience of time, as accompanies motherhood. "Vertiginous.... Denying the reader any orienting poles for the projected reality.... McSweeney's breakneck prose harnesses the throbbing pulse of language itself." (**PUBLISHERS WEEKLY**) "Biological, morbid, fanatic, surreal, McSweeney's impulses are to go to the rhetoric of the maternity mythos by evoking the spooky, sinuous syntaxes of the gothic and the cleverly constructed political allegory. At its core is the proposition that writing the mother-body is a viscid cage match with language and politics in a declining age.... This collection is the sexy teleological apocrypha of motherhood literature, a siren song for those mothers 'with no soul to photograph.'" (**THE BROOKLYN RAIL**) "Language commits incest with itself.... Sounds repeat, replicate, and mutate in her sentences, monstrous sentences of aural inbreeding and consangeous consonants, strung out and spinning like the dirtiest double-helix, dizzy with disease...." (**QUARTERLY WEST**)

JENNY BOULLY
NOT MERELY BECAUSE OF THE UNKNOWN THAT WAS STALKING TOWARD THEM

"This is undoubtedly the contemporary re-treatment that Peter Pan deserves.... Simultaneously metaphysical and visceral, these addresses from Wendy to Peter in lyric prose are scary, sexual, and intellectually disarming." (*HUFFINGTON POST*) In her second SPD Bestseller from Tarpaulin Sky Press, *not merely because of the unknown that was stalking toward them*, Jenny Boully presents a "deliciously creepy" swan song from Wendy Darling to Peter Pan, as Boully reads between the lines of J. M. Barrie's *Peter and Wendy* and emerges with the darker underside, with sinister and subversive places. *not merely because of the unknown* explores, in dreamy and dark prose, how we love, how we pine away, and how we never stop loving and pining away. "To delve into Boully's work is to dive with faith from the plank — to jump, with hope and belief and a wish to see what the author has given us: a fresh, imaginative look at a tale as ageless as Peter himself." (*BOOKSLUT*) "Jenny Boully is a deeply weird writer—in the best way." (*ANDER MONSON*)

MORE FICTION, NONFICTION, POETRY
& HYBRID TEXTS FROM TARPAULIN SKY PRESS

FULL-LENGTH BOOKS

Jenny Boully, *[one love affair]**

Ana Božičević, *Stars of the Night Commute*

Traci O. Connor, *Recipes for Endangered Species*

Mark Cunningham, *Body Language*

Danielle Dutton, *Attempts at a Life*

Sarah Goldstein, *Fables*

Johannes Göransson, *Entrance to a colonial pageant in which we all begin to intricate*

Johannes Göransson, *Haute Surveillance*

Noah Eli Gordon & Joshua Marie Wilkinson, *Figures for a Darkroom Voice*

Dana Green, *Sometimes the Air in the Room Goes Missing*

Gordon Massman, *The Essential Numbers 1991 - 2008*

Joyelle McSweeney, *Nylund, The Sarcographer*

Kim Parko, *The Grotesque Child*

Joanna Ruocco, *Man's Companions*

Kim Gek Lin Short, *The Bugging Watch & Other Exhibits*

Kim Gek Lin Short, *China Cowboy*

Shelly Taylor, *Black-Eyed Heifer*

Max Winter, *The Pictures*

David Wolach, *Hospitalogy*

Andrew Zornoza, *Where I Stay*

CHAPBOOKS

Sandy Florian, *32 Pedals and 47 Stops*
James Haug, *Scratch*
Claire Hero, *Dollyland*
Paula Koneazny, *Installation*
Paul McCormick, *The Exotic Moods of Les Baxter*
Teresa K. Miller, *Forever No Lo*
Jeanne Morel, *That Crossing Is Not Automatic*
Andrew Michael Roberts, *Give Up*
Brandon Shimoda, *The Inland Sea*
Chad Sweeney, *A Mirror to Shatter the Hammer*
Emily Toder, *Brushes With*

G.C. Waldrep, *One Way No Exit*

Tarpaulin Sky Literary Journal
in print and online

tarpaulinsky.com

CPSIA information can be obtained
at www.ICGtesting.com
Printed in the USA
FSHW011630070520
69813FS